P9-AQT-210

Bathtime Buddies

WITHDRAWN
No longer the property of the
Boston Public Library.
Sale of this material benefits the Library

Bathtime Buddies

20 Crocheted Animals from the Sea

Megan Kreiner

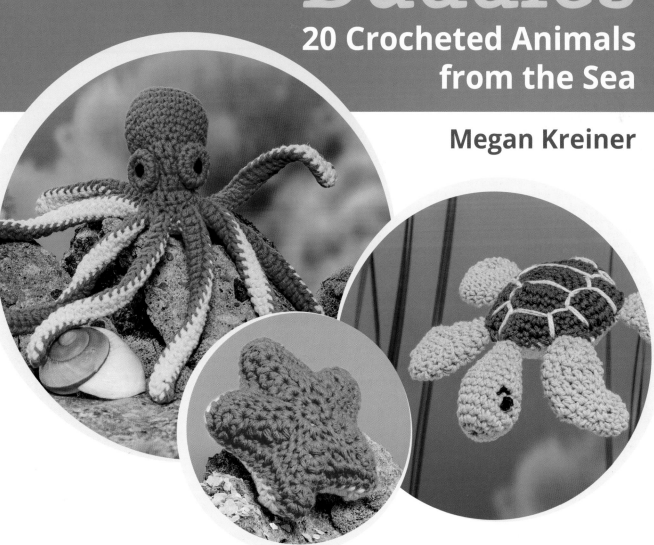

Martingale®

Create with Confidence

Dedication

For my two bathing beauties, James and Emily

Bathtime Buddies:
20 Crocheted Animals from the Sea
© 2014 by Megan Kreiner

Martingale®
19021 120th Ave. NE, Ste. 102
Bothell, WA 98011-9511 USA
ShopMartingale.com

No part of this product may be reproduced in any form, unless otherwise stated, in which case reproduction is limited to the use of the purchaser. The written instructions, photographs, designs, projects, and patterns are intended for the personal, noncommercial use of the retail purchaser and are under federal copyright laws; they are not to be reproduced by any electronic, mechanical, or other means, including informational storage or retrieval systems, for commercial use. Permission is granted to photocopy patterns for the personal use of the retail purchaser. Attention teachers: Martingale encourages you to use this book for teaching, subject to the restrictions stated above.

The information in this book is presented in good faith, but no warranty is given nor results guaranteed. Since Martingale has no control over choice of materials or procedures, the company assumes no responsibility for the use of this information.

Printed in China

19 18 17 16 15 14   8 7 6 5 4 3 2 1

Library of Congress Cataloging-in-Publication Data is available upon request.

ISBN: 978-1-60468-415-5

MISSION STATEMENT

Dedicated to providing quality products and service to inspire creativity.

CREDITS

PRESIDENT AND CEO: Tom Wierzbicki

EDITOR IN CHIEF: Mary V. Green

DESIGN DIRECTOR: Paula Schlosser

MANAGING EDITOR: Karen Costello Soltys

ACQUISITIONS EDITOR: Karen M. Burns

TECHNICAL EDITOR: Ursula Reikes

COPY EDITOR: Marcy Heffernan

PRODUCTION MANAGER: Regina Girard

COVER AND INTERIOR DESIGNER: Connor Chin

PHOTOGRAPHER: Brent Kane

ILLUSTRATORS: Sue Mattero, Cheryl Fall, and Megan Kreiner

Contents

THE PROJECTS

Introduction

Splish splash, crochet in the bath! Bath time is fun time at our house, and a tub filled with bubbles seems to inspire all kinds of imaginative play.

As a follow-up to *Crochet a Zoo* (Martingale, 2013), this new collection of under-the-sea creatures is full of techniques to make soft water-loving bath toys (along with tips to make the same toys for land use only) using kid-friendly materials and baby-safe options.

I had a whale of a time putting these patterns together, and I hope you'll enjoy making a whole tub full of sea creatures for bath time or playtime in your home!

Tools and Materials

If you're just getting started with crochet, this section is for you. When it comes to materials for your first crochet projects, always keep in mind quality over quantity. You don't need much yarn to make these toys, so it's worth using the best-quality materials for your special projects.

YARN AND GAUGE

Choosing a yarn for your project is part of the fun of personalizing your creation! It's always a good idea to keep the age of your recipient in mind when choosing what kind of yarn to use. For very young children who like to put everything in their mouths, it might be prudent to go with organic or natural fibers, such as cotton or wool (but always be sure to check for allergies first).

Yarn for Bath Toys

For projects that are destined to end up in the tub, cotton yarns or cotton blends (like cotton/hemp, cotton/bamboo, or cotton/acrylic) hold up well to spending time in hot water. You'll want to seek out yarns that have a fairly soft feel to make them gentler on skin.

Yarn for Non-Bath Toys

If your toy is meant to stay on dry land, then your yarn options will be much broader. Blended yarns are wonderful, as they often combine the best qualities of their respective fibers. Acrylic yarns can also make excellent toys, as they are fairly easy to clean and care for and are generally less expensive than natural-fiber yarns.

Gauge

To adjust the size of a toy, choose a lighter or heavier weight yarn. For example, if you wish to make a family of dolphins, you could use sport- or DK-weight yarn and a size D-3 (3.25 mm) or E-4 (3.5 mm) hook to make a smaller version of the original, or go jumbo with your blue whale by using bulky-weight yarn and a size I-9 (5.5 mm) hook. Refer to the standard yarn-weight chart on page 92 for more information.

Some of the toys in this book use patterns for cutting pieces from fabric to sew onto the crocheted toys. You may need to adjust the size of the patterns accordingly to accommodate the smaller or larger finished toy sizes if you adjust your gauge.

Most of the projects in this book call for worsted-weight yarn and a size F-5 (3.75mm) hook, but you may find that the gauge of worsted-weight yarns can vary quite a bit in thickness from one brand to the next. Feel free to adjust your hook size accordingly so that your stitches stay close together. It's always better to err on the side of caution by going with a smaller hook since you want your stitches to be fairly tight to prevent the stuffing from showing through.

As a general rule, 125 yards of worsted-weight yarn should be more than enough to make one toy.

STUFFING

Options for stuffing vary depending on whether you're making a bath or non-bath toy.

For Bath Toys

All the bath toys in this book are stuffed with 1" cubes of sponge cut from an infant bath sponge mat. One sponge mat produced enough stuffing for about four toys. (See "Resources" on page 93.) As a bonus, the bath sponge is mildew resistant to help keep your toys clean between dunkings and cleanings.

I recommend avoiding cellulose sponges (or sponges cut from dehydrated sponge sheets) to stuff your toys. These kinds of sponges have a tendency to dry out and harden, which can make the toy a bit crunchy when dry.

See page 23 for tips on caring for and drying your bath toys.

Summer Infant Comfy Bath Sponge, cut into small pieces, makes great stuffing for bath toys.

For Non-Bath Toys

As with yarns, you can choose from a variety of toy stuffings. Most craft and fabric stores carry polyester fiberfill, although more locations now carry natural fiber and organic options as well. The Internet can be a great resource for specialty toy stuffing, such as organic wool and organic cotton. Check out the resources page (page 93) for where you can find organic and natural stuffing.

Fiberfill, cotton, and wool toy stuffings (from left to right)

Sadly, black stuffing for dark-colored toys seems to be a rather scarce commodity, and—unless your stitches are super tight—white stuffing tends to show through, which can be an undesirable look. For black and brown toys, we have other options.

- An old black T-shirt cut up into little pieces can make effective stuffing. And it's thrifty!

- If you don't require too much black stuffing, you could use black wool roving. It may be a bit pricey, but it can be a good way to go if you wish to use only natural or organic materials in your project.

- Turn black cotton batting, like Hobbs Bonded Fibers Heirloom 80/20 Black Cotton Blend Quilt Batting, into stuffing. Simply cut off a chunk of batting and brush the heck out of it with a pet grooming slicker brush. The result is clumps of black fluffiness that can then be used in your toy. It's a bit of work, but the result is pretty effective. Just make sure you place a scrap cloth under the batting before you start brushing so you don't scratch your work surface. If you don't have a brush handy, you can also use scissors to cut the batting into little ½" to 1" pieces.

- Around Halloween you may come across a product called Halloween Hay from Polyester Fibers, which is essentially black polyester fiberfill. If you find it, stock up!

NOISEMAKERS (FOR NON-BATH TOYS)

To add a little more zing to your toy, you can also purchase noisemakers like bells, squeakers, or rattles to insert into the body of your sea creature.

Noisemakers from American Felt and Craft

CROCHET HOOKS

Crochet hooks vary in size, color, and material. I prefer metal hooks, because they're strong and don't bend while stitching. If you can, hold the hooks in your hand before you make your purchase to ensure a comfortable fit.

If you find your hand feels sore after crocheting for an extended period of time, it may be worth checking out the various lines of ergonomic hooks.

Assortment of crochet hooks. Notice that the ergonomic ones have a wider grip than traditional crochet hooks.

For the most accurate sizing, go by the millimeter sizing on the hook since different manufacturers use a range of markings and systems like numbers or letters. (See "Crochet Hook Sizes" on page 92.) I used an F-5 (3.75 mm) hook for the projects in this book. Because you're making stuffed animals and not garments, your stitch gauge and overall sizing is not crucial. Just be sure you're crocheting a firm fabric that won't allow stuffing to show through.

STITCH COUNTERS AND SLIP RINGS

Most of these patterns are worked in a continuous spiral. A stitch or row counter, combined with the use of slip rings or safety pins marking the beginning of each round, can help you keep track of which round you are currently working on. You can also use slip rings to hold the edges of two crochet pieces together as you sew an edge closed.

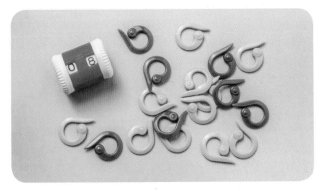

Keep track of your progress easily with the help of stitch markers and a row/stitch counter.

STICKY NOTES AND PENCILS

I always keep a small stack of sticky notes and a mechanical pencil in my notions bag. That way, when I need to stop midway through a project, I can stick a note right on the page in my pattern book and jot down exactly where I left off in the pattern. I'll sometimes just draw an arrow on the sticky note and line up the arrow with my current row so I can easily find my place when I come back to my project.

PLASTIC EYES WITH SAFETY BACKINGS (FOR NON-BATH TOYS)

Plastic eyes with safety backings are available at craft stores and on the Internet. My favorite online resource is Etsy shop 6060, where you can pick up a variety of hard-to-find sizes and colors. The plastic backings, once applied, are designed not to accidentally come off again. However, for children under three, I strongly recommend using felt circles or French knots for eyes (see page 18), as the plastic eyes can become a choking hazard if removed.

For bath toys, stick with French knots for all your toys. Check out page 18 for tips on how to bulk up your French knots.

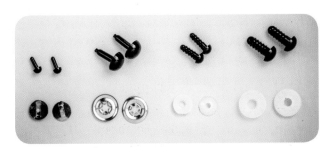

A variety of plastic safety eyes from Etsy shop 6060

TERRY CLOTH, FELT, AND THREAD

Several projects have features that require fabric and thread.

Sea creatures with terry cloth and felt patch options

Terry Cloth

For bath toys, I used washcloth material or terry cloth for the sea-creature patches. You can find a variety of terry-cloth colors at fabric stores or online. In a pinch, most patterns will also fit on a standard washcloth if you only need a small amount of material to work with.

Terry cloth from Fabrics.com

Using the illustration for reference, secure the patches to the body using pins; sew the patches in place using an appliqué stitch (page 19) and cotton thread.

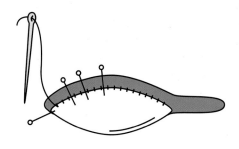

Felt

For non-bath toys, you can use terry cloth as well, but my material of choice is usually felt. Craft felt comes in a variety of colors and fiber contents, such as polyester, acrylic, wool, and bamboo. If using wool and bamboo felt, you can either hand wash your toys in cool water or prewash your felt before cutting out and attaching the pieces to your toy, making the final toy machine washable. You can choose thread that matches your felt, or you can go for a fun patchwork look and use a contrasting color.

A selection of wool and bamboo felt from American Felt and Craft, organic threads from NearSea Naturals, and traditional cotton threads from Gütermann

When tracing shapes onto felt, I find that a ballpoint pen or blunted No. 2 pencil works fairly well on light colors, while a white gel pen works best on darker colors. Cut inside the lines so the marks will not show, or you can turn the piece over. For making felt eyes, you can use the various holes in a knitting needle gauge to trace the perfect eye sizes down to the millimeter.

For felt belly patches, sew the darts as marked before securing the patch to the body with pins. Sew the patches in place with a running stitch (page 19) and cotton thread.

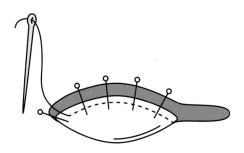

CUTTING TOOLS

Consider investing in a high-quality pair of scissors for cutting out terry-cloth and felt shapes, and a smaller pair of embroidery scissors for trimming threads and loose ends. Regardless of what brand you choose, use these scissors only on your crocheted projects to keep the blade nice and sharp.

STEEL TAPESTRY NEEDLES

A few steel tapestry needles will make assembling your sea creatures a snap. Skip the plastic tapestry needles, since they can sometimes bend when going through thick materials like felt or a tightly stuffed toy. Sew finished toy parts and open edges together and make French-knot eyes using a large tapestry needle (size 13) with worsted-weight yarn, or a smaller tapestry needle (size 17) with DK- or sport-weight yarn. For easier threading, look for needles with big eyes.

A size 20 or 22 embroidery or chenille needle is good for sewing on eyes and embroidering other details.

STRAIGHT PINS

Straight pins with round glass heads can be a huge help in holding all your toy's pieces together before sewing everything in place. In addition, the pins will help hold the folded edges of your patches down while stitching. I like the ones with big round heads so they're easy to handle.

Crochet Stitches

This section will provide an overview of all the stitches used for the patterns in this book. Since most of the patterns use only a few basic stitches, they make great projects for beginners.

SLIPKNOT

1 Make a loop with your yarn, leaving a 6" tail.

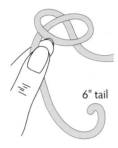

6" tail

2 Insert the hook into the loop and gently pull up and tighten the yarn around the hook. The tail will be woven into your finished piece.

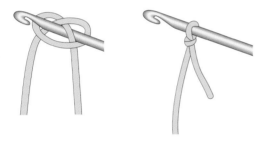

YARN OVER

Wrap the yarn over your hook from back to front.

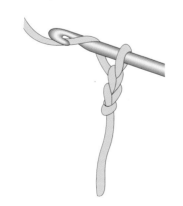

FOUNDATION CHAIN (ch)

Make a slipknot and place it on your hook. You'll have one loop on your hook.

1 Yarn over the hook with the working yarn.

2 Catch the yarn with your hook and draw it through the loop on your hook. You will now have a new loop on your hook with the slipknot below it. This is your first or "foundation" chain.

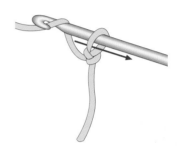

3 Repeat steps 1 and 2 to make as many chains as indicated in the pattern. When checking your count, keep in mind that you should skip the loop currently on the hook and only count the chains below it.

SLIP STITCH (sl st)

Slip stitches can be used to move yarn across multiple stitches without adding additional height to the row. Start by inserting your hook into the next chain or stitch, yarn over the hook, and pull through both loops on the hook in one motion. You'll have one remaining loop on your hook.

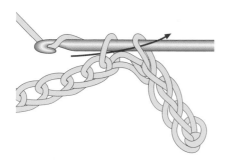

SINGLE CROCHET (sc)

❶ Insert your hook into the indicated chain or stitch in the pattern, yarn over the hook, and pull through the chain or stitch. You'll have two loops on your hook.

❷ Yarn over the hook and pull through both loops on your hook to complete the stitch. You'll have one loop on your hook.

HALF DOUBLE CROCHET (hdc)

❶ Yarn over the hook and insert the hook into the indicated chain or stitch in the pattern. Yarn over the hook and pull through the chain or stitch. You'll have three loops on your hook.

❷ Yarn over the hook and pull through all three loops on the hook to complete the stitch. You'll have one loop on your hook.

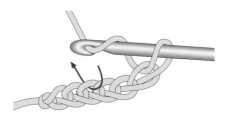

DOUBLE CROCHET (dc)

❶ Yarn over the hook and insert the hook into the indicated chain or stitch in the pattern.

❷ Yarn over the hook and pull through the chain or stitch. You'll have three loops on your hook.

❸ Yarn over the hook and pull through two loops on the hook. You'll have two loops remaining on the hook.

❹ Yarn over the hook and pull through the last two loops on the hook to complete the stitch. You'll have one loop on your hook.

TRIPLE CROCHET (tr)

❶ Yarn over the hook twice and insert the hook into the indicated chain or stitch in the pattern. Yarn over the hook and pull through the chain or stitch. You'll have four loops on your hook.

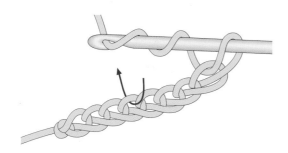

❷ Yarn over the hook and pull through two loops on the hook. You'll have three loops on your hook.

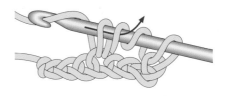

❸ Yarn over the hook and pull through two loops on the hook. You'll have two loops on your hook.

❹ Yarn over the hook and pull through the last two loops on the hook to complete the stitch. You'll have one loop on your hook.

SINGLE-CROCHET INCREASES

You'll see most of the patterns in this book indicate "sc 2 in next sc" when an increase is needed. To work an increase, simply work the number of stitches specified into the same stitch.

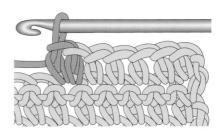

SINGLE-CROCHET DECREASES (sc2tog)

All the patterns in this book use single-crochet decreases.

❶ Insert your hook into the next stitch, yarn over the hook, and pull through the stitch, leaving a loop on your hook. You'll have two loops on your hook.

❷ Repeat step 1 in the next stitch. You'll have three loops on your hook.

❸ Yarn over the hook and pull through all three loops. You'll have one loop on your hook.

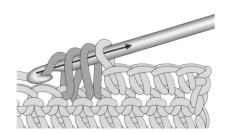

INVISIBLE SINGLE-CROCHET DECREASE (sc2tog)

This technique can be used instead of the standard single-crochet decrease. It helps eliminate the spaces that sometimes appear in the surface of your toy as you make your decreases.

❶ Insert your hook into the front loop of the next stitch and then immediately into the front loop of the following stitch. You will have three loops on your hook.

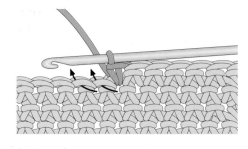

❷ Yarn over and draw the working yarn through the two front loops on the hook. You'll have two loops on your hook.

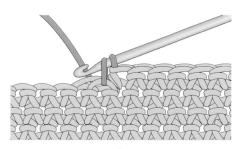

❸ Yarn over the hook and pull through both loops on your hook to complete the stitch. You'll have one loop on your hook.

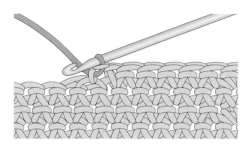

WORKING IN A SPIRAL ROUND

The projects in this book are worked in a spiral round in which there are no slip stitches or chains between rounds. Just keep crocheting from one round to the next. It can be helpful to use stitch markers and row counters.

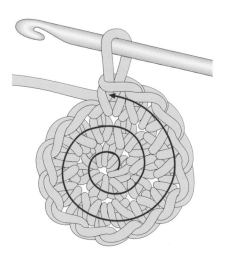

To keep track of the round you are currently on, place a stitch marker in the last stitch of the round you just worked. You'll know you've come to the end of a round when you get to the stitch with the marker. After removing the marker, work the last stitch in the round, replace the marker in the new last stitch, and proceed to the first stitch of the next round.

ADJUSTABLE RING

The adjustable ring is a great technique that can take care of the unsightly hole in the middle of your starting round.

1 Form a ring with your yarn, leaving a 6" tail. Insert the hook into the loop as shown, as if you were making a slipknot.

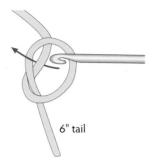

6" tail

2 Yarn over the hook and pull through the loop to make a slip stitch.

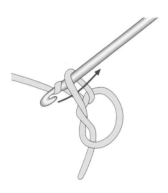

3 Chain one and then single crochet the number of stitches indicated in the pattern, taking care to enclose both strands of yarn that make up the adjustable ring. To close the center of the ring, pull tightly on the 6" yarn tail. Your adjustable ring is now complete.

To start the next round, work your next stitch in the first single crochet of the adjustable ring. If you need to make a semicircle shape (like for an ear or fin), you'll be instructed to chain one and turn the work so that the wrong side of the work is facing you. You can then crochet into the single-crochet stitches of the adjustable ring as indicated in the pattern.

WORKING AROUND A CHAIN

A few patterns begin by working around a chain of stitches. After creating your chain, you'll first work in the back ridge loops of the chain and then in the front loops of the chain.

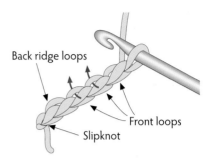

Back ridge loops
Front loops
Slipknot

1 Make a chain as per the pattern instructions. The first chain stitch after the slipknot will be your "foundation chain."

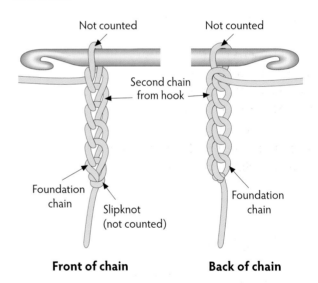

Not counted   Not counted
Second chain from hook
Foundation chain
Slipknot (not counted)
Foundation chain

Front of chain   **Back of chain**

2 For round 1, starting in the second chain from the hook, work your first stitch in the back ridge loop of the chain. Continue working the pattern into the back ridge loops of the chain until you've reached the back ridge loop of the first foundation chain.

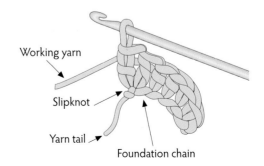

Working yarn
Slipknot
Yarn tail
Foundation chain

❸ When you're ready to work the other side of the chain, rotate your work so the front loops are facing up. Starting in the next chain from the foundation chain, insert your hook under the two front loops of the chain stitch to work your stitch.

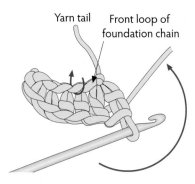

Yarn tail   Front loop of foundation chain

Rotate and work in front loops of chain.

❹ Continue in the pattern until you reach the first stitch of round 1. You can now fasten off your yarn to complete the shape. For patterns that instruct you to continue on to round 2, work your next stitch into the first stitch of round 1.

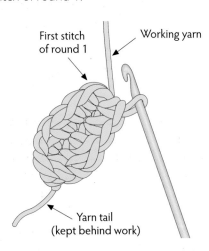

First stitch of round 1

Working yarn

Yarn tail (kept behind work)

CHECKING YOUR STITCH COUNT

Occasionally, you may want to count the stitches on your current round to make sure you have the correct number as you're going along. The basic rule of thumb to remember is that the loop on the hook does not count as a stitch.

RIGHT SIDE (RS) VERSUS WRONG SIDE (WS)

It's important to keep track of which side of your pattern is the right side, as it will affect which part of the stitch you'll perceive as the back loop versus the front

loop. Since most of the pattern pieces begin with an adjustable ring, the 6" tail left over from forming the ring will usually lie on the wrong side of the piece. The same can be said for patterns started by working around a chain, if you take care to keep the 6" yarn tail behind your work as you crochet.

BACK LOOPS (BL) AND FRONT LOOPS (FL)

Unless otherwise indicated, you'll be working in both loops of a stitch except when the pattern instructs that a stitch should be worked in the back loop or front loop only. When viewing your piece from the right side, the back loop will be the loop farthest away while the front loop is the loop closest to you.

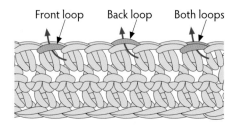

Front loop   Back loop   Both loops

FASTENING OFF

After you've completed your last stitch, cut the yarn, leaving at least a 6" tail. To fasten the yarn off, draw this tail through the last loop on your hook and pull firmly to secure it. In many cases, you can use the long tail to sew other pieces to the body or to sew up a seam.

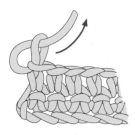

CHANGING COLORS

Changing colors requires a little reading ahead, since a new color is actually introduced while you are completing the last stitch of the old color.

Work the stitch prior to the color change up to the last step in which you would normally pull the yarn through the loop(s) on your hook to complete the stitch. Proceed to swap out your old color for a new color and draw the new color through your loop(s) to complete the stitch. The result will be a loop of the new color on your hook. You can then continue on to the next stitch in the new color.

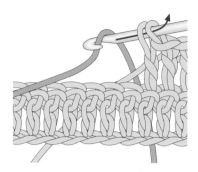

When introducing a second color, leave at least a 6" yarn tail that you can tie to the first yarn color on the wrong side of the work to avoid any gaps caused by loose strands at the site of the color change.

CROCHETING ON THE SURFACE

Crocheting on the surface of your piece is a great way to add texture to animals like seahorses. Patterns that call for this technique will use it in a very free-form kind of way so that the stitches are simply placed wherever you think they should go.

❶ On the right side of your work, insert your hook through the surface stitch of your piece, yarn over the hook and draw a loop back out through the surface stitch. You'll have one loop on your hook.

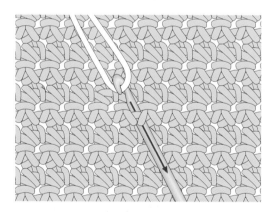

❷ Insert your hook into a space very close to your starting point and draw out another loop of yarn through the surface of your piece. You'll have two

loops on your hook. Yarn over the hook in preparation for making the single crochet in the next step.

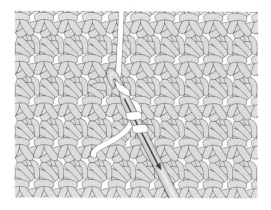

❸ Pull the yarn through the two loops. You've just made a single crochet on the surface of your piece.

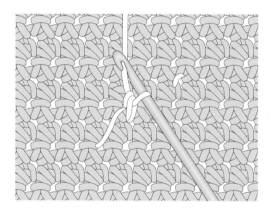

❹ Repeat steps 2 and 3 to create a free-form line of single crochet along the surface of your piece. Depending on the pattern instructions, you may continue to work additional rows into these stitches. Fasten off and weave in ends when finished.

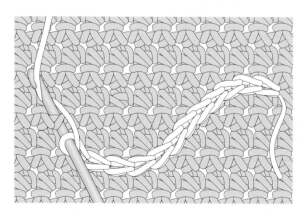

Sewing and Embroidery Stitches

Simple embroidery stitches are useful for adding eyes, eyebrows, gills, and fabric pieces like terry cloth and felt.

BACKSTITCH

The backstitch can be used to create simple line details on the surface of a toy.

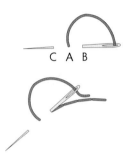

LAZY DAISY STITCH

To create a pleasing curved eyebrow, I like to use a variation of the lazy daisy stitch. Draw the yarn and needle through the surface of your work at point A where you would like the arch or eyebrow to begin. Reinsert the needle where you would like the arch to end at point B and very loosely draw the needle through the work. Make small adjustments to the loose yarn on the surface to form a nice arch. To secure the arched shape, draw the needle through at the top of the arch at point C and back down through the surface at point D, making a small stitch to hold the arch in place.

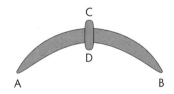

FRENCH KNOT

French-knot eyes are ideal for bath-safe toys and can be used in place of plastic safety eyes.

With the yarn and needle on the right side of the work, hold the yarn close to the surface of the work where the yarn has most recently emerged and wind the yarn around the needle four or five times (depending on how big an eye you would like to make). While still applying tension to the yarn, insert the needle close to where the yarn has most recently emerged. Pull the needle through the work, leaving a knot on the surface.

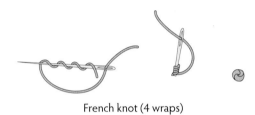

French knot (4 wraps)

To bulk up the French knot, draw the needle and yarn out at the base of the completed French knot and proceed to wind the yarn around the base of the French knot three or four times.

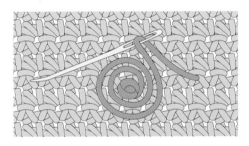

To secure, draw the needle through the top surface of the French knot to catch a few loops and pull tightly.

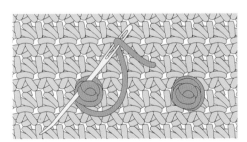

RUNNING STITCH

Use a running stitch to sew on felt eye circles and felt belly patches. Simply pass the needle and thread in and out of the fabric in a dashed-line pattern.

LONG STITCH

A long stitch can be used for shaping the surface of your toy. Pass the needle in and out of the fabric at whichever distance is needed as per the assembly instructions for the piece. To shape or cinch the surface of the toy, loop the long stitch back to the starting location and repeat two or three times while pulling tightly.

APPLIQUÉ STITCH

An appliqué stitch is used to secure the folded edge of a terry-cloth patch to the surface of your toy. After folding and securing the patch to the toy with pins, bring the needle and thread up through the surface of the toy and catch the folded edge of the patch. Insert the needle through the toy surface close to where the needle caught the folded fabric edge. Repeat these steps as you continue around the folded edge.

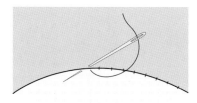

Finishing Touches

For the best results when putting your toy together, follow these final tips.

WHIPSTITCH

The whipstitch is useful for closing seams in a nice neat line and for sewing your creature together. To close the openings on fins and flippers, pinch the open edges together with your fingers. Using your tapestry needle and leftover yarn tail, draw the needle and yarn through your piece making sure to catch both edges. Pull the yarn up and over the edge of the work before pulling the needle through both edges again, in a spiral-like motion. Continue until the seam is closed or the piece is attached.

CLOSING HOLES

For closing round holes like the ones on heads and body shapes, thread the remaining yarn tail onto a tapestry needle. Following the edge of the opening, insert the needle through each space and over the next single crochet, effectively winding the tail around the stitches. When you've worked all the way around the opening, pull the tail firmly to close the hole (just like you were cinching a drawstring bag closed).

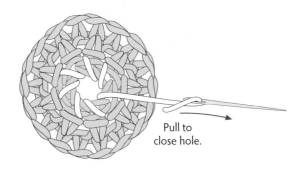

Pull to close hole.

ATTACHING BODY PARTS

After you've closed up your seams, you can begin to assemble your toy! For fins and flippers, lay the closed seams flat against the body and whipstitch them in place with the leftover yarn tail. If you find it tricky to keep the fin placement even, use a couple of large straight pins to pin your fins into position to make sure your placement will work before you start sewing everything in place.

To attach pieces that have open-ended edges (like the muzzle on the otter), join the pieces to the surface of the body by whipstitching all around the open edge to attach them.

SECURING YARN ENDS

It can become a pesky business dealing with attaching, tying off, and sewing in yarn ends when applying embroidery stitches. To make things a bit easier, try this trick. Starting with a new piece of yarn, insert your needle about an inch from where you intend to start your embroidery and leave a 4" tail. Bring the needle up at the first stitch. Hold the yarn tail down with your fingers as you work the first couple of stitches until the yarn appears to feel secure. When you finish your last stitch, bring the needle out at the same spot of the beginning tail and cut the end, leaving another 4" tail. Knot the two yarn tails together, and then use a crochet hook or tapestry needle to draw the yarn and the knot back through the hole. It might take a bit of a tug to pull the knot and yarn tails through, but everything will be nicely hidden.

EYE OPTIONS

Knowing who the recipient of the toy will be will help you determine which eye option is most suitable.

French Knots

Little embroidered knots add a nice textural element to your toy's face, while fatter French knots achieve a look close to that of the plastic eyes, but are a safer option for children under three. They're also the recommended option for any toy that you are making for the bath. See page 18 for instructions on how to make these cute little knots.

Plastic Eyes

Plastic eyes are a great option for non-bath toys meant for children over three years old. A great bonus of using plastic eyes is that you can easily move them around the face (prior to securing the backings). Try different sizes to determine what will work the best on your toy.

Installing Safety Backing

Be prepared to remove some stuffing from your toy when installing the safety backing on the eyes. You can use your crochet hook to help pull the stuffing out. From the outside of your toy, push the eye close to the opening in your toy until you can feel the post. Then install the backing and restuff.

Felt Circles

Eye patterns are on page 87. They match the diameters of the various plastic eyes used in this book. A small pair of sewing scissors or cuticle scissors will make cutting out these little circles easier. Attach the felt circles using thread and a running stitch (page 19), or with fabric glue.

Tip

Use a knitting-needle gauge and white gel pen on black felt to trace perfectly sized eyes.

LINING THEM UP

To ensure the sea creature's eyes and body parts end in the right spot, look over the finishing illustrations and photos for each toy before you begin assembling them. The illustrations will help you with the final placement of your animal's features, and the project steps will provide clear instruction regarding spacing. Consider keeping a stash of pins handy to help mark the placement of your various animal parts before sewing everything together.

USING TEMPLATES

You can make templates for the sewn-on patches using tracing paper or a photocopier/scanner, or by downloading and printing them from ShopMartingale .com/extras or MKCrochet.com/resources.

Cutting and Appliquéing Terry-Cloth Shapes

❶ Cut out the traced or printed template using the solid black lines as a guide. Pin the template to terry cloth, and cut out the fabric. Using scissors, clip into the terry cloth ¼" from the edge around the perimeter of the piece.

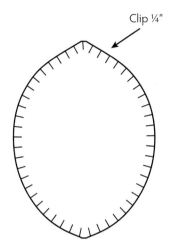

Clip ¼"

❷ Using the clips as a guide and with the right side of the fabric facing out, fold the edges under and pin the appliqué patch to the surface of your toy. Using the appliqué stitch (page 19) and a needle and thread, sew the folded edge to the crocheted surface.

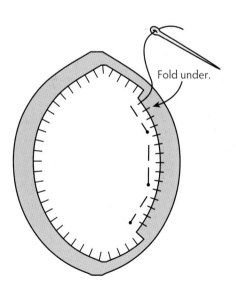

Fold under.

Cutting and Applying Felt Shapes

For felt shapes or fabrics that don't need to have the edges turned under, cut out the template using the dotted line as a guide. For edges that are sewn together to form darts for shaping, pin those edges together and sew them using a whipstitch on the wrong side of the felt patch before sewing the patch to the toy.

Pinning method: This method is best if you only need to cut out one piece for your project. If you need more than two pieces, see "Printer or Copier," right. Place the tracing paper over the pattern and trace the shape onto the paper with a pencil. Loosely cut out the traced pattern leaving about a ¼" border around the shape. Cut out a square of felt large enough to accommodate the pattern. Use a few straight pins to secure the template to the felt. Proceed to cut out the shape.

Taping method: Using packing tape, tape the template in place so that both the tracing paper and the felt are covered. You can double up the felt if you need two of the same shape, but make sure the tape folds around the felt stack just enough to hold it together (taking care to not cover the bottom of the second piece of felt with tape). The tape will not be removed easily from the felt once it sticks.

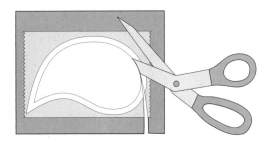

I don't recommend using your best fabric scissors for this method, as the tape will leave a sticky residue on the blades. If you need to clean your scissor blades, a little Goo Gone (sold at craft stores) will take off the tape residue.

Tracing Tip

Here's a nifty little trick using Glad Press 'n Seal. Unroll a piece of this plastic wrap large enough to cover the pattern. Place it tacky side down on top of the pattern, then trace around it with a pencil or pen. Pull the plastic off the paper and stick it onto the felt. Cut out the shape, peel off the plastic wrap, and you're good to go!

Printer or Copier

Print the pattern you need using either a computer scanner or a copy machine. You can also resize a pattern easily using this method, if desired. You can also download and print out the various patterns from ShopMartingale.com/extras or MKCrochet.com/resources. To transfer the patterns to felt, use one of these options:

- Cut out the pattern with scissors and trace it onto the felt using either a ballpoint pen or a pencil on light-colored felt and a white gel pen on dark felt.

- Cut out the pattern with scissors, leaving a ¼" border and staple it to the felt. Cut out the shape, and then remove the staples. If you need multiples of the same shape, you can stack a few pieces of felt beneath the template.

- Print the pattern onto cardstock and create a stencil by cutting out the shapes using a utility craft knife and a cutting mat. Applying firm pressure, hold the stencil down on top of the felt and carefully cut out the felt shape using the stencil as a guide. This works best when the utility knife has a fresh blade.

Double Threading a Needle

Here's a trick for when you want a little extra thread strength when sewing your felt shapes onto the sea creatures.

❶ Cut a piece of thread twice as long as you normally would need for sewing around the shape.

❷ Fold the thread in half and insert both ends into the eye of the sewing needle to create a big loop.

❸ Pass the needle in and out of the surface of your toy, pulling the thread partially through until there is only a 2" or 3" loop of thread left at the surface of your work. Stop pulling and guide your needle through this small loop. Pull gently to tighten the loop and secure your needle and thread.

❹ Once your thread is secured you can then sew on your felt patch with the doubled thread. For kids' toys, I think this method is a bit more robust since they can't easily pull the thread out, and as a bonus, you don't need to knot or fasten off the thread at the beginning.

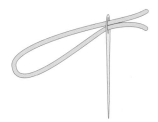

Caring for Your Toys

The following guidelines will help keep your toys clean.

WASHING NON-BATH TOYS

I recommend hand washing for most toys (especially if the toy has plastic eyes or felt details) in cool or luke-warm water. Detergents and gentle soaps like Soak or Woolite will do a good job cleaning your crocheted toy. After washing your toy in soapy water, you'll need to rinse the soap out before rolling the toy up in a towel to help gently wring out the extra water. Allow the toy to air dry in a well-ventilated area.

For toys that don't have felt patches or plastic eyes, you could give the washer and dryer a go if the care instructions on the yarn you've used will allow for it. Place the toy in a lingerie bag, clean it on a gentle cycle in your washer, and then dry it in the dryer on low heat or allow it to air dry.

You want to be as gentle as possible when cleaning your toys to ensure that the shaping and details are preserved.

SANITIZING BATH TOYS

Place the toys containing sponges in the washing machine to help keep them sanitized. If you wish, you can place them in a lingerie bag to help keep them protected during the washing cycle.

DRYING YOUR BATH TOYS

Do not place bath toys in the hot dryer to dry as this can melt the sponges inside. Ring out your toys as best you can and store them in a hanging mesh bag to air dry in a well-ventilated area. You can also crochet a small chain of 20 stitches and attach it to your sea creature as a loop. You can then hang your toy from this loop on a hooked suction cup placed on the wall next to your tub to help dry your toy in between bath times. If you place them on the counter, you might find they take longer to dry. If you want to speed up the process, you can also try drying them in a lingerie bag in a dryer set to "air dry" (no heat).

Starfish

These roly-poly sea stars are quick to make and look pretty cute floating around in a bubble bath. If you'd like to add a special surprise to the underside of your starfish, you can make a happy face by adding French knot eyes and a little lazy daisy mouth using black yarn

Skill Level: Beginner ◣□□□▷   **Finished Size:** Approx 4" wide and 1" tall

MATERIALS

MC Worsted-weight yarn in bright color of your choice (approx 25 yds)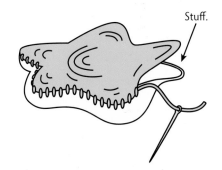

CC Worsted-weight yarn in cream (approx 25 yds)

Worsted-weight yarn in black (approx 2 yds)

Size F-5 (3.75 mm) crochet hook

Tapestry needle

Sponge stuffing for bath toys or toy stuffing for non-bath toys

Stitch markers to indicate beginning of rnds (optional)

BODY

Make 1 in MC and 1 in CC.

Make a 5-st adjustable ring (page 14).

Rnd 1: Sc 3 in each st around. (15 sts)

Rnd 2: *Sl st, hdc 3 in next sc, sl st; rep from * 4 more times. (25 sts)

Rnd 3: *Sl st, sc 1, hdc 3 in next hdc, sc 1, sl st; rep from * 4 more times. (35 sts)

Rnd 4: *Sl st 2, sc 1, hdc 3 in next hdc, sc 1, sl st 2; rep from * 4 more times. (45 sts)

Rnd 5: *Sl st 4, hdc 3 in next hdc, sl st 4; rep from * 4 more times. (55 sts)

Rnd 6: *Sc 5, sc 3 in next hdc, sc 5; rep from * 4 more times. (65 sts)

Fasten off. For MC, leave an extra-long tail.

ASSEMBLY

Line up top and bottom body pieces with WS tog. Use slip ring or safety pins to hold edges tog while you whipstitch them closed with MC yarn tail. Stuff before closing.

Stuff.

Guppies

Mix-and-match guppies! These cute little guys are quick and easy to make and you can choose from a variety of fin and tail shapes to customize your fish to your liking.

Skill Level: Beginner ●□□□ **Finished Size:** Approx 4" long and 3" tall

MATERIALS

MC Worsted-weight yarn in bright color of your choice (approx 25 yds)

CC Worsted-weight yarn in contrasting bright color of your choice (approx 25 yds)

Worsted-weight yarn in black (approx 2 yds)

Size F-5 (3.75 mm) crochet hook

Tapestry needle

Sponge stuffing for bath toys

For non-bath toys: 8 mm or 9 mm black plastic eyes with safety backings and toy stuffing (see "Resources," page 93)

Stitch markers to indicate beginning of rnds (optional)

BODY

Using MC, make an 8-st adjustable ring (page 14).

Rnd 1: Sc 2 in each sc around. (16 sts)

Rnd 2: *Sc 3, sc 2 in next sc; rep from * 3 more times. (20 sts)

Rnds 3–7: Sc 20.

Rnd 8: *Sc 3, sc2tog; rep from * 3 more times. (16 sts)

Rnd 9: *Sc 2, sc2tog; rep from * 3 more times. (12 sts)

Rnd 10: *Sc 1, sc2tog; rep from * 3 more times. (8 sts)

Stuff body.

Rnd 11: *Sc 2, sc2tog; rep from * 1 more time. (6 sts)

Fasten off, leaving a long tail. If you're not using plastic eyes, close 6-st hole and weave in end.

SIDE FINS

There are 3 side fin options.

Half-Circle Side Fin

Make 2.

Using CC, make a 3-st adjustable ring. Ch 1 and turn.

Sk first ch, sc 2 in each sc. (6 sts)

Fasten off, leaving a long tail.

Small-Drop Side Fin

Make 2.

Using CC, loosely ch 4.

Starting in 2nd ch from hook and working in back ridge lps, sc 1, hdc 1, dc 3 in back ridge lp of next ch. Rotate work. Starting in next ch and working in front lps, hdc 1, sc 1.

Fasten off, leaving a long tail.

Small-Fan Side Fin

Make 2.

Using CC, make a 3-st adjustable ring. Ch 1 and turn.

Sk first ch, sc 1, hdc 3 in next sc, sc 1. (5 sts)

Fasten off, leaving a long tail.

TAIL FINS

There are 4 tail fin options.

Teardrop Tail Fin

Make 2.

Using CC, loosely ch 6.

Starting in 2nd ch from hook and working in back ridge lps, sc 2, hdc 2, dc 5 in back ridge lp of next ch. Rotate work. Starting in next ch and working in front lps, hdc 2, sc 2.

Fasten off, leaving a long tail.

Half-Circle Tail Fin

Make 1.

Using CC, make a 3-st adjustable ring. Ch 1 and turn.

Row 1: Sk first ch, sc 2 in each sc. Ch 1 and turn. (6 sts)

Row 2: Sk first ch, sc 2 in each sc. (12 sts)

Fasten off, leaving a long tail.

WHICH FINS TO MAKE?

Orange body: Wave fins (back and belly), flame tail, small-drop side fins (pointy end facing out)

Yellow body: Ruffle and half-circle fins (back and belly), scallop tail, half-circle side fins

Light-blue body: Spike (back and belly), half-circle tail, small-drop side fins (pointy end facing in)

Lavender body: Half-circle fin (back), teardrop tail (make two and attach the larger ends to the back of the fish to make a fish tail), small-fan side fins

Flame Tail Fin

Make 1.

Using CC, make a 7-st adjustable ring.

Rnd 1: Sc 2 in next 3 sc, (hdc 1, dc 1, tr 1, dc 1, hdc 1) in next sc, sc 2 in next 3 sc. (17 sts)

Rnd 2: Sl st 8, (sc 1, hdc 1, dc 1, hdc 1, sc 1) in next sc, sl st 8. (21 sts)

Fasten off, leaving a long tail.

Scalloped Tail Fin

Make 1.

Using CC, make a 3-st adjustable ring. Ch 1 and turn.

Row 1: Sk first ch, sc 1, hdc 3 in next sc, sc 1, ch 1 and turn. (5 sts)

Row 2: Sk first ch, sc 1, hdc 2 in next 3 sc, sc 1, ch 1 and turn. (8 sts)

Row 3: Sk first ch, *(sl st, hdc 1, dc 1, hdc 1, sl st) in next st, sk next st; rep from * 3 more times. (20 sts)

Fasten off, leaving a long tail.

BACK AND BELLY FINS

There are 4 fin options.

Half-Circle Fin

Make 1 or 2.

Work as for "Half-Circle Side Fin" on page 27.

Spike Fin

Make 1 or 2.

Using CC, loosely ch 6.

Starting in 2nd ch from hook and working in back ridge lps, sc2tog, hdc 1, dc 1, tr 1.

Fasten off, leaving a long tail.

Wave Fin

Make 1 or 2.

Using CC, loosely ch 11.

Starting in 2nd ch from hook and working in back ridge lps, sl st, sc2tog, sc 1, hdc 1, dc 2, tr 2, (dc 1, hdc 1, sc 1) in back ridge lp of next ch.

Fasten off, leaving a long tail.

Ruffle Fin

Make 1 or 2.

Using CC, loosely ch 7.

Starting in 2nd ch from hook and working in back ridge lps, *(sl st, hdc 1, dc 1, hdc 1, sl st) in next ch, sk next ch; rep from * 2 more times. (20 sts)

Fasten off, leaving a long tail.

ASSEMBLY

Using black yarn, apply French knots (page 18) to sides of head. For non-bath toys, attach plastic eyes or sew on felt circles. With black yarn, embroider eyebrows above eyes using a lazy daisy st (page 18). Close 6-st hole and weave in end. Using CC, attach side fins, tail fins, and back and belly fins.

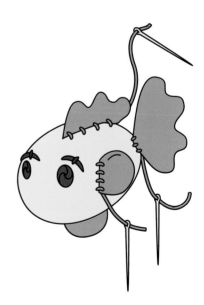

Stingray

This stingray sports a tail of the non-stinging variety. With eyes at the top of its head and a flat body, it can easily hide under the sandy bottom of the ocean or under a layer of suds in a bathtub while still keeping a lookout for what's going on up above.

Skill Level: Easy ◖■☐▢   **Finished Size:** Approx 7" long and 4" wide

MATERIALS

Worsted-weight yarn in taupe (approx 25 yds) ()
Worsted-weight yarn in cream (approx 25 yds)
Worsted-weight yarn in black (approx 5 yds)
Size F-5 (3.75 mm) crochet hook
Tapestry needle
Sponge stuffing for bath toy
For non-bath toy: 8 mm or 9 mm black plastic eyes with safety backings and toy stuffing
Stitch markers to indicate beginning of rnds (optional)

BODY

Make 1 in taupe yarn and 1 in cream yarn.

Loosely ch 6.

Rnd 1: Starting in 2nd ch from hook and working in back ridge lps, sc 4, sc 5 in back ridge lp of next ch. Rotate work. Starting in next ch and working in front lps, sc 3, sc 4 in next ch. (16 sts)

Rnd 2: Sc 4, *hdc 2 in next sc; rep from * 3 more times, sc 4, **hdc 2 in next sc; rep from ** 3 more times. (24 sts)

Rnds 3 and 4: Sc 24.

Rnd 5: Sc 2 in each sc around. (48 sts)

Rnd 6: Sc 3, hdc 2, dc 2, tr 2, dc 2, hdc 2, sc 3, sl st 8, sc 3, hdc 2, dc 2, tr 2, dc 2, hdc 2, sc 3, sl st 5, ch 16. Starting in 2nd ch from hook and working in back ridge lps, sc 4, hdc 8, dc 3, sl st 3 in last 3 st of rnd 5.

Fasten off, leaving a long tail.

ASSEMBLY

1 Place RS of cream belly piece against WS of taupe back body. With cream side facing you and using taupe yarn, sew body pieces tog using backstitch (page 18) to create a solid line of taupe sts on belly side of stingray between rnds 4 rnd 5. Leave space in the seam at the end for stuffing.

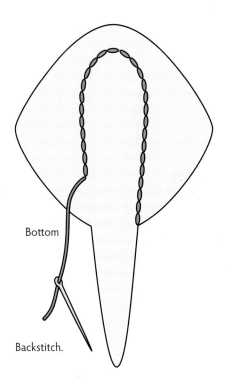

Bottom

Backstitch.

2 With taupe side facing up, apply plastic eyes for non-bath toys. For bath-safe toys, use black yarn and apply French knots (page 18) for eyes. With black yarn, embroider eyebrows above eyes using lazy daisy st (page 18). Stuff center section and finish backstitch.

4 Using black yarn, apply 3 short sts to each side of belly for gills.

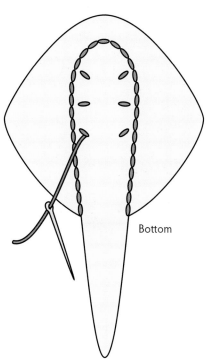

Bottom

Stuff.

3 With taupe yarn, whipstitch top and bottom outside edges tog.

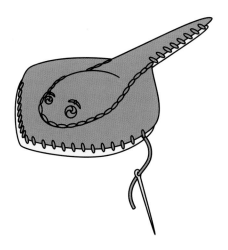

Jellyfish

These jellyfish are a great project for using up any variegated cotton yarn you might have floating around your house. It's the perfect yarn for jellyfish tentacles! You also have the option to make your jellyfish body solid or patterned depending on which body you choose. To make the tentacles extra spirally, just twist them around your fingers before letting them loose for a swim.

Skill Level: Easy ◐■□□   **Finished Size:** Approx 3" wide and 9" long

MATERIALS

For patterned jellyfish body

MC Worsted-weight yarn in a light color (approx 25 yds)

CC Worsted-weight yarn in a dark color (approx 25 yds)

For solid jellyfish body

Worsted-weight yarn (approx 50 yds)

For both

Worsted-weight yarn in a complementary variegated color (approx 100 yds)

Size F-5 (3.75 mm) crochet hook

Tapestry needle

Sponge stuffing for bath toys or toy stuffing for non-bath toys

Stitch markers to indicate beginning of rnds (optional)

PATTERNED BODY

Using MC, make an 8-st adjustable ring (page 14).

Rnd 1: Sc 2 in each sc around. (16 sts)

Rnd 2: *Sc 3, sc 2 in next sc; rep from * 3 more times. (20 sts)

Switch to CC, do NOT cut MC.

Rnd 3: *Sc 1, sc 2 in next sc; rep from * 9 more times. (30 sts)

Rnd 4: *Sc 4, switch to MC, sc 2 in next sc, switch to CC; rep from * 5 more times. (36 sts)

Rnd 5: *Sc2tog 2 times, switch to MC, **sc 2 in next sc; rep from ** 1 more time, switch to CC; rep from * 5 more times. (36 sts)

Rnd 6: * Sc2tog, switch to MC, sc 3, sc 2 in next sc, switch to CC; rep from * 5 more times. (36 sts)

Rnds 7 and 8: *Sc 1, switch to MC, sc 5, switch to CC; rep from * 5 more times. (36 sts)

Switch to MC.

Rnd 9: Sc 36.

Rnd 10: *Sc 4, sc2tog; rep from * 5 more times. (30 sts)

Switch to CC.

Rnd 11: *Sc 1, sc2tog; rep from * 9 more times. (20 sts)

Rnd 12: In fl, *dc 5 in next sc, sl st; rep from * 9 more times. (60 sts)

Switch to MC.

Rnd 13: Sc 60.

Fasten off and weave in end.

SOLID BODY

Using MC, make an 8-st adjustable ring.

Rnd 1: Sc 2 in each sc around. (16 sts)

Rnd 2: *Sc 3, sc 2 in next sc; rep from * 3 more times. (20 sts)

Rnd 3: *Sc 1, sc 2 in next sc; rep from * 9 more times. (30 sts)

Rnd 4: *Sc 4, sc 2 in next sc; rep from * 5 more times. (36 sts)

Rnds 5–9: Sc 36.

Rnd 10: *Sc 4, sc2tog; rep from * 5 more times. (30 sts)

Switch to CC.

Rnd 11: *Sc 1, sc2tog; rep from * 9 more times. (20 sts)

Rnd 12: In fl, *dc 5 in next sc, sl st; rep from * 9 more times. (60 sts)

Switch to MC.

Rnd 13: Sc 60.

Fasten off and weave in end.

BELLY AND TENTACLES

Make 1.

Using variegated yarn, make a 5-st adjustable ring.

Rnd 1: Sc 2 in each sc around. (10 sts)

Rnd 2: Sc 2 in each sc around. (20 sts)

Rnd 3 (make tentacles): *Sc 1 in next sc, loosely ch 30 to 40 sts; this long ch will stick out like a spoke from belly of jellyfish. Starting in 2nd ch from hook and working in back ridge lps, sc 2 in each ch. When you get to end of ch, sc 1 in next sc of rnd 2; rep from * 9 more times with chains of various lengths between 30 to 40 sts for each tentacle.

Fasten off, leaving a long tail. Twist each tentacle around your finger to help shape the corkscrew.

ASSEMBLY

Using yarn tail and running stitch, attach belly and tentacles to open edge of body with RS facing out, taking care to sew edge of belly to rnd 11 on body in order to keep ruffle loose. Stuff body before closing seam.

Optional Jellyfish Face

If you would like to add a face, apply plastic eyes or felt circles for non-bath toys, or black yarn and French knots (page 18) for bath toys, to jellyfish body before closing up body seam. With black yarn, embroider eyebrows above eyes using lazy daisy st (page 18).

Stuff.

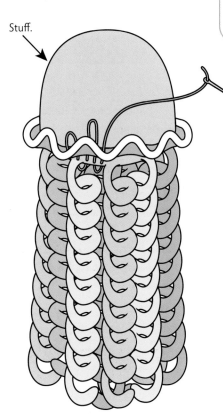

Seahorse

These seahorses come complete with curly tails to keep them from drifting away in rough waters. My favorite factoid about seahorses is that the males carry the developing seahorse babies in special pouches within their abdomens. I designed this pattern during the seventh month of my second pregnancy and thought that the seahorse arrangement of who has to carry the baby around sounded like a pretty sweet deal.

Skill Level: Easy ◗■□□ **Finished Size:** Approx 1½" wide and 6" tall

MATERIALS

MC Worsted-weight yarn in a bright color (approx 30 yds)

CC Worsted-weight yarn in a contrasting bright or variegated color (approx 10 yds)

Worsted-weight yarn in black (approx 5 yds)

Size F-5 (3.75 mm) crochet hook

Tapestry needle

Sponge stuffing for bath toys

For non-bath toys: 8 mm or 9 mm black plastic eyes with safety backings and toy stuffing

Stitch markers to indicate beginning of rnds (optional)

HEAD

Using MC, make an 8-st adjustable ring (page 14).

Rnd 1: In bl, sc 8.

Rnd 2: Sc2tog 4 times. (4 sts)

Rnds 3 and 4: Sc 4.

Rnd 5: Sc 2 in each sc around. (8 sts)

Rnd 6: Sc 8.

Rnd 7: *Sc 1, sc 2 in next sc; rep from * 3 more times. (12 sts)

Rnd 8: *Sc 1, sc 2 in next sc; rep from * 5 more times. (18 sts)

Rnd 9: Sc 18.

Rnd 10: *Sc 1, sc2tog; rep from * 5 more times. (12 sts)

Rnd 11: Sc 12.

Rnd 12: *Sc 1, sc2tog; rep from * 3 more times. (8 sts)

Stuff head.

Rnd 13: *Sc 2, sc2tog; rep from * 1 more time. (6 sts)

Fasten off, leaving a long tail.

BODY

Using MC, make a 4-st adjustable ring.

Rnds 1–12: Sc 4.

Rnd 13: *Sc 1, sc 2 in next sc; rep from * 1 more time. (6 sts)

Rnds 14–16: Sc 6.

Rnd 17: *Sc 2, sc 2 in next sc; rep from * 1 more time. (8 sts)

Rnd 18: Sc 8.

Rnd 19: *Sc 1, sc 2 in next sc; rep from * 3 more times. (12 sts)

Rnd 20: Sc 12.

Rnd 21: *Sc 1, sc 2 in next sc; rep from * 5 more times. (18 sts)

Rnd 22: Sc 18.

Rnds 23–25: Sc 3, hdc 3, dc 6, hdc 3, sc 3. (18 sts)

Rnd 26: Sc2tog 2 times, sc 2, hdc 6, sc 2, sc2tog 2 times. (14 sts)

Rnd 27: Sc2tog 2 times, sc 6, sc2tog 2 times. (10 sts)

Stuff body.

Rnd 28: *Sc 3, sc2tog; rep from * 1 more time. (8 sts)

Fasten off, leaving a long tail.

FIN

Make 2.

Using MC, make a 4-st adjustable ring. Ch 1 and turn.

Sk first ch, sc 2 in each sc. (8 sts)

Fasten off, leaving a long tail.

ASSEMBLY

1 Using black yarn, apply French knots (page 18) to sides of head. For non-bath toys, attach plastic eyes or sew on felt circles. With black yarn, embroider eyebrows above eyes using lazy daisy st (page 18). Close 6-st hole and weave in end. Using MC, attach head to open end at top of body.

If needed, add a few sts between the chin and chest to angle head downward.

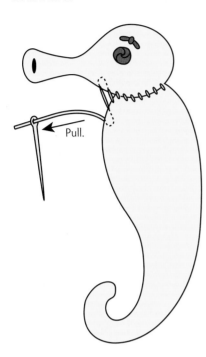

Row 2: Sk first ch, *(sc 1, hdc 1, sc 1) in next sc, sl st; rep from * to last sc of row 1 at top of head. Fasten off.

❸ Attach fins on either side of ruffle.

❹ Starting at end of tail, use MC to sew 2" or 3" of running sts (page 19) to inside surface of tail. Pull yarn tightly before fastening off to curl tail.

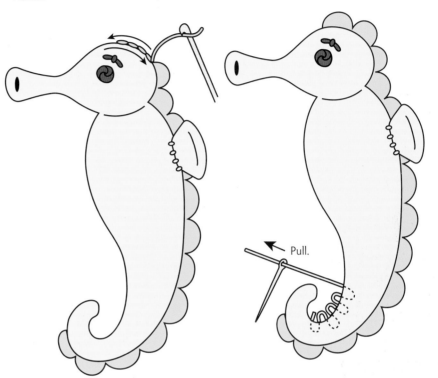

❷ Add ruffle to back as follows.
Row 1: Using CC, sc an even number of sts onto surface of seahorse (see "Crocheting on the Surface," page 17) starting at top of head and working down back to about 1" from end of tail. Ch 1 and turn.

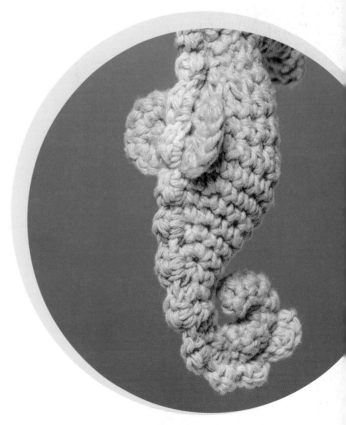

Sea Turtle

This little sea turtle is a cruiser and likes nothing more than a relaxing swim. In the ocean, a sea turtle's shell helps it blend into its environment because it is dark on top and lighter on the bottom. So, whether you were to look down from above at the dark surface of the ocean or were under water looking up at the brighter sky, our little turtle's shell would be harder to see from either direction.

Skill Level: Easy ◼◼◻◻   **Finished Size:** Approx 5" tall and 7" long

MATERIALS

Worsted-weight yarn in light green (approx 50 yds)
Worsted-weight yarn in dark green (approx 25 yds)
Worsted-weight yarn in cream (approx 25 yds)
Worsted-weight yarn in black (approx 5 yds)
Size F-5 (3.75 mm) crochet hook
Tapestry needle
Sponge stuffing for bath toy
For non-bath toy: 8 mm or 9 mm black plastic eyes with safety backings and toy stuffing
Straight pins
Stitch markers to indicate beginning of rnds (optional)

HEAD

Using light-green yarn, make a 6-st adjustable ring (page 14).

Rnd 1: Sc 2 in each st around. (12 sts)

Rnd 2: *Sc 1, sc 2 in next sc; rep from * 5 more times. (18 sts)

Rnd 3: *Sc 8, sc 2 in next sc; rep from * 1 more time. (20 sts)

Rnds 4–6: Sc 20.

Rnd 7: *Sc 3, sc2tog; rep from * 3 more times. (16 sts)

Rnd 8: *Sc 6, sc2tog; rep from * 1 more time. (14 sts)

Rnd 9: *Sc 5, sc2tog; rep from * 1 more time. (12 sts)

Rnd 10: Sc 12.

Stuff head.

Rnd 11: *Sc 1, sc2tog; rep from * 3 more times. (8 sts)

Rnds 12 and 13: Sc 8.

Fasten off, leaving a long tail. Do not close seam.

FRONT FLIPPER

Make 2.

Using light-green yarn, make a 5-st adjustable ring.

Rnd 1: Sc 2 in each sc around. (10 sts)

Rnd 2: Sc 3, hdc 4, sc 3. (10 sts)

Rnd 3: Sl st 3, hdc 4, sl st 3. (10 sts)

Rnd 4: Sl st 3, hdc 1, *hdc 2 in next st; rep from * 1 more time, hdc 1, sl st 3. (12 sts)

Rnd 5: Sl st 3, hdc 2, *hdc 2 in next st; rep from * 1 more time, hdc 2, sl st 3. (14 sts)

Rnds 6–8: Sl st 3, hdc 2, dc 4, hdc 2, sl st 3. (14 sts)

Rnd 9: Sc 14.

Rnd 10: *Sc 5, sc2tog; rep from * 1 more time. (12 sts)

Rnd 11: *Sc 1, sc2tog; rep from * 3 more times. (8 sts)

Rnd 12: Sc 8.

Rnd 13: *Sc 2, sc2tog; rep from * 1 more time. (6 sts)

Fasten off, leaving a long tail. Do not stuff.

BACK FLIPPER

Make 2.

Using light-green yarn, make a 6-st adjustable ring.

Rnd 1: Sc 3, sc 2 in next sc, sc 3 in next sc, sc 2 in next sc. (10 sts)

Rnd 2: Sc 3, *sc 2 in next sc; rep from 6 more times. (17 sts)

Rnds 3–5: Sc 17.

Rnd 6: Sc2tog, *sc 1, sc2tog; rep from * 4 more times. (11 sts)

Rnd 7: Sc 1, *sc 3, sc2tog; rep from * 1 more times. (9 sts)

Rnd 8: Sc 9.

Rnd 9: *Sc 1, sc2tog; rep from * 2 more times. (6 sts)

Rnd 10: Sc 6.

Fasten off, leaving a long tail. Do not stuff.

SHELL

Make 1 in dark-green yarn and 1 in cream yarn.

Make a 6-st adjustable ring.

Rnd 1: Sc 2 in each st around. (12 sts)

Rnd 2: *Sc 1, sc 2 in next sc; rep from * 5 more times. (18 sts)

Rnd 3: *Sc 2, sc 2 in next sc; rep from * 5 more times. (24 sts)

Rnd 4: *Sc 3, sc 2 in next sc; rep from * 5 more times. (30 sts)

Rnd 5: *Sc 4, sc 2 in next sc; rep from * 1 more time, hdc 4, hdc 3 in next sc, hdc 4, sc 2 in next sc, **sc 4, sc 2 in next sc; rep from ** 1 more time. (37 sts)

Rnd 6: Sc 12, hdc 6, dc 3 in next st, hdc 6, sc 12. (39 sts)

Rnd 7: Sc 12, hdc 7, dc 3 in next st, hdc 7, sc 12. (41 sts)

Fasten off, leaving a long tail.

ASSEMBLY

❶ Using black yarn, apply French knots (page 18) to sides of head. For non-bath toys, attach plastic eyes or sew on felt circles. With black yarn, embroider eyebrows above eyes using lazy daisy st (page 18).

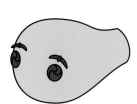

❷ With WS of cream shell facing up, position flippers and head around edge of shell with about 2 rnds of overlap. Using cream yarn and running st (page 19), sew around inside perimeter of shell to attach pieces.

❸ Place top shell over bottom shell so WS face each other. Using dark-green yarn, whipstitch edges of top and bottom shells tog, sandwiching limbs and head between 2 shell pieces as you sew. Stuff before closing seam.

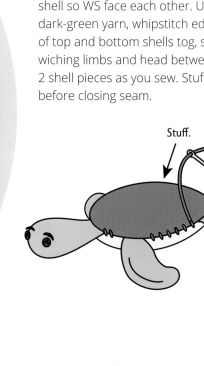

Stuff.

4 **Shell detail:** Place 4 pins through center of top shell, evenly spaced (A). Thread 2 strands of cream yarn on tapestry needle and, following illustration, make 4 horizontal long sts (page 19) across back of shell referring to pins for spacing. Reposition 2 pins between each pair of horizontal sts a bit beyond ends of sts (B). Using the cream yarn, st from ends of each long st to pins, creating a column of 3 hexagonal boxes along back of shell (C). To complete pattern, make long sts from outside corners of hexagonal boxes to edges of shell, taking care to check symmetry of pattern as you embroider (D).

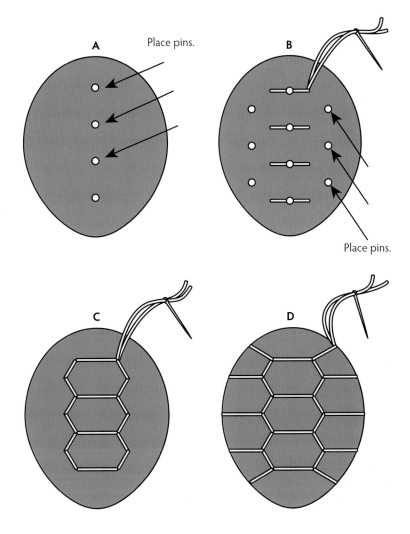

A   Place pins.   B

Place pins.

C   D

Angler Fish

This angler pattern came out a bit more goofy than scary in my opinion. Looking at pictures of real angler fish could give anyone a few bad dreams. The angler gets its glow from bioluminescent bacteria that resides in the tip of the angler's lure. If you happen to be technically savvy (and not making a bath toy), you could install an LED in your angler's lure to make a cool, light-up reading light. Check out "LED clip-on earrings" on Amazon.com if you're feeling adventurous.

Skill Level: Easy ⬤◼☐☐   **Finished Size:** Approx 5" long, 4" tall

MATERIALS

Worsted-weight yarn in fuchsia (100 yds)
Worsted-weight yarn in black (20 yds)
Worsted-weight yarn in cream (15 yds)
Size F-5 (3.75 mm) crochet hook
Tapestry needle
Sponge stuffing for bath toy
For non-bath toy: 8 mm or 9 mm black plastic eyes with safety backings and toy stuffing
Stitch markers to indicate beginning of rnds (optional)

BODY

Using fuchsia yarn, make an 8-st adjustable ring (page 14).

Rnd 1: Sc 2 in each sc around. (16 sts)

Rnd 2: *Sc 3, sc 2 in next sc; rep from * 3 more times. (20 sts)

Rnd 3: *Sc 1, sc 2 in next sc; rep from * 9 more times. (30 sts)

Rnd 4: *Sc 4, sc 2 in next sc; rep from * 5 more times. (36 sts)

Rnds 5–9: Sc 36.

Rnd 10: *Sc 4, sc2tog; rep from * 5 more times. (30 sts)

Rnd 11: Sc 30.

Rnd 12: *Sc 1, sc2tog; rep from * 9 more times. (20 sts)

Rnd 13: Sc 20.

Rnd 14: *Sc 3, sc2tog; rep from * 3 more times. (16 sts)

Rnd 15: Sc 16.

Rnd 16: Sc2tog 8 times. (8 sts)
Stuff head.

Rnd 17: *Sc 2, sc2tog; rep from * 1 more time (6 sts).

Fasten off, leaving a long tail. If you're not using plastic eyes, close 6-st hole and weave in end.

MOUTH

Using black yarn, make a 6-st adjustable ring.

Rnd 1: Sc 2 in next sc, hdc 2 in next sc, sc 2 in next 2 sc, hdc 2 in next sc, sc 2 in next sc. (12 sts)

Rnd 2: Sc 2 in next 2 sc, hdc 2 in next 2 sts, sc 2 in next 4 sts, hdc 2 in next 2 sts, sc 2 in next 2 sc. (24 sts)

Rnd 3: Sc 4, hdc 4, sc 8, hdc 4, sc 4. (24 sts)

Switch to fuchsia yarn to form lip.

Rnd 4: In fl, hdc 24. (24 sts)

Rnd 5: In bl, hdc 2 in each st around. (48 sts)

Fasten off, leaving a long tail.

SIDE FIN AND TAIL

Make 3.

Using fuchsia yarn, make a 3-st adjustable ring. Ch 1 and turn.

Row 1: Sk first ch, sc 1, hdc 3 in next sc, sc 1. Ch 1 and turn. (5 sts)

Row 2: Sk first ch, sc 1, hdc 2 in next 3 sc, sc 1. (8 sts)

Fasten off, leaving a long tail.

DORSAL FIN

Using fuchsia yarn, loosely ch 5. Starting in 2nd ch from hook and working in back ridge lps, sc 1, hdc 2 in next 2 sts, sc 1. Fasten off.

LURE

Using fuchsia yarn, make an 8-st adjustable ring.

Rnd 1: In bl, *sc 2, sc2tog; rep from * 1 more time. (6 sts)

Rnd 2: Sc 6.

Rnd 3: *Sc 1, sc2tog; rep from * 1 more time. (4 sts)

Rnds 4–11: Sc 4.

Rnd 12: In fl, sc 2 in each sc around. (8 sts)

Rnd 13: Sc 8.

Switch to cream yarn.

Rnd 14: In bl, sc 8.

Rnd 15: *Sc 2, sc2tog; rep from * 1 more time. (6 sts)

Stuff lure lightly.

Rnd 16: *Sc 1, sc2tog; rep from * 1 more time. (4 sts)

Fasten off, leaving a long tail. Close 4-st hole and weave in end.

ASSEMBLY

❶ Fold fuchsia lip edge back toward body and sew in place using fuchsia yarn to form a rounded lip. Sew mouth to rounder end of body using whipstitch (page 20).

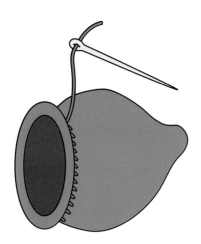

❷ Thread tapestry needle with fuchsia yarn. Shape nose bridge by making a long st (page 19) 10 to 12 sts wide through top of body directly behind top of lip. Pull tightly and rep 2 or 3 times. On either side of mouth, loop a 1"-long st through lip at sides of mouth 2 or 3 times, pulling tightly to pinch and shape corners of mouth.

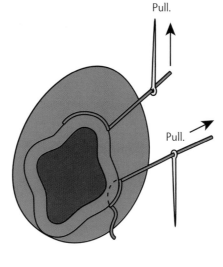

Pull.

Pull.

❸ Using black yarn, apply French knots (page 18) to sides of nose bridge just above top of mouth. For non-bath toys, attach plastic eyes or sew on felt circles. With black yarn, embroider eyebrows above eyes using lazy daisy st (page 18). Close 6-st hole and weave in end.

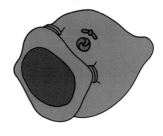

❹ Using fuchsia yarn, attach one fin to each side of body and remaining fin to back of body for a tail. Attach base of lure to top center of head a few rnds behind eyes. Attach dorsal fin to back of body between lure and tail.

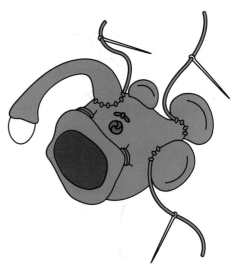

❺ Thread 2 strands of cream yarn on a tapestry needle and embroider teeth onto black portion of mouth using long sts.

Octopus

Octopuses or octopi. Whatever you call them, they do some pretty neat tricks. They can change colors, learn to use tools, and since they don't have skeletons, can fit into the tiniest cracks and spaces. It's up to you what tricks you'd like to teach your octopus.

Skill Level: Easy ◼◼◻◻   **Finished Size:** Approx 8" long and 3" wide

MATERIALS

Worsted-weight yarn in orange red (approx 100 yds)

Worsted-weight yarn in cream (approx 75 yds)

Worsted-weight yarn in black (5 yds)

Size F-5 (3.75 mm) crochet hook

Tapestry needle

Sponge stuffing for bath toy

For non-bath toy: 8 mm or 9 mm black plastic eyes with safety backings and toy stuffing

Stitch markers to indicate beginning of rnds (optional)

BODY AND TENTACLES

Using orange-red yarn, make an 8-st adjustable ring (page 14).

Rnd 1: Sc 2 in each sc. (16 sts)

Rnd 2: *Sc 3, sc 2 in next sc; rep from * 3 more times. (20 sts)

Rnd 3: *Sc 1, sc 2 in next sc; rep from * 9 more times. (30 sts)

Rnd 4–8: Sc 30.

Rnd 9: *Sc 1, sc2tog; rep from * 9 more times. (20 sts)

Rnd 10: Sc 20.

Rnd 11: Dc 5, *sc 3, sc2tog; rep from * 2 more times. (17 sts)

Rnd 12: Dc 6, sc 3, sc2tog, sc 1, sc2tog, sc 3. (15 sts)

Rnd 13: Dc 6, sc 2, sc2tog, sc 1, sc2tog, sc 2. (13 sts)

Rnd 14: Dc 6, sc 2, *sc 2 in next sc; rep from * 2 more times, sc 2. (16 sts)

Rnd 15 (make tentacles): *Sc 1 in next sc, ch 25. Starting in 3rd ch from hook and working in back ridge lps, dc 3, dc 22 to end of ch, sc 1 in next sc of rnd 14; rep from * 7 more times.

Fasten off, leaving a long tail.

BELLY AND TENTACLES

Using cream yarn, make an 8-st adjustable ring.

Rnd 1: *Sc 1, sc 2 in next sc; rep from * 3 more times. (12 sts)

Rnd 2: *Sc 2, sc 2 in next sc; rep from * 3 more times. (16 sts)

Rnd 3 (make tentacles): *Sc 1 in next sc, ch 25. Starting in 3rd ch from hook and working in back ridge lps, dc 3, dc 22 to end of ch, sc 1 in next sc of rnd 2; rep from * 7 more times.

Fasten off, and weave in end.

EYE BASE

Make 2.

Using orange-red yarn, make a 6-st adjustable ring.

Rnd 1: Sc 2 in each sc. (12 sts)

Rnds 2 and 3: Sc 12.

Rnd 4: Sc2tog 6 times. (6 sts)

Do not stuff. Fasten off, leaving a long tail.

ASSEMBLY

1 Place belly and body with WS tog so tentacle edges match up for easier sewing. Hold edges tog with slip rings or safety pins. Using orange-red yarn, whipstitch edges tog around each of the tentacles and where belly edge meets body edge, but do not close seam entirely (leave a 1" opening at the end). Stuff body.

2 Sew open edges of eye bases to sides of head. Using black yarn, apply French knots (page 18) to centers of each eye base. For non-bath toys, attach plastic eyes or sew on felt circles to centers of eye bases. For plastic eyes, the plastic posts will go through both eye base and into octopus body before applying the safety backing. Once eyes are secure, close body seam.

Stuff.

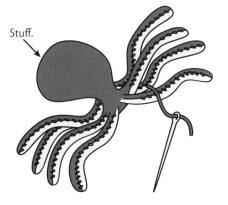

Manatee

It's suspected that early tales of mermaids were actually sightings of manatees by sailors who had obviously been away from land a wee bit too long. Your sweet and gentle manatee may not win any beauty contests, but you can always add some long flowing hair and a seashell bra from the mermaid pattern in this book if you really want to gussy up your sea cow!

Skill Level: Easy ⬛◼◻◻   **Finished Size:** Approx 7" long and 3" tall

MATERIALS

Worsted-weight yarn in gray (approx 125 yds)
Worsted-weight yarn in black (approx 5 yds)
Size F-5 (3.75 mm) crochet hook
Tapestry needle
Sponge stuffing for bath toy
For non-bath toy: 8 mm or 9 mm black plastic eyes with safety backings and toy stuffing
Stitch markers to indicate beginning of rnds (optional)

TAIL

Using gray yarn, make an 8-st adjustable ring (page 14).

Rnd 1: Sc 2 in each sc. (16 sts)

Rnd 2: *Sc 1, sc 2 in next sc; rep from * 7 more times. (24 sts)

Rnd 3: Sc 24.

Rnd 4: *Sc 3, sc 2 in next sc; rep from * 5 more times. (30 sts)

Rnds 5–7: Sc 30.

Rnd 8: *Sc 3, sc2tog; rep from * 5 more times. (24 sts)

Rnd 9: *Sc 1, sc2tog; rep from * 7 more times. (16 sts)

Rnd 10: Sc2tog 8 times. (8 sts)

Fasten off. Flatten seam and sew closed, leaving a long tail.

BODY

Using gray yarn, make an 8-st adjustable ring.

Rnd 1: Sc 2 in each sc around. (16 sts)

Rnd 2: *Sc 3, sc 2 in next sc; rep from * 3 more times. (20 sts)

Rnd 3: *Sc 1, sc 2 in next sc; rep from * 9 more times. (30 sts)

Rnds 4–6: Sc 30.

Rnd 7: *Sc 4, sc 2 in next sc; rep from * 5 more times. (36 sts)

Rnds 8–10: Sc 36.

Rnd 11: *Sc 4, sc2tog; rep from * 5 more times. (30 sts)

Rnds 12 and 13: Sc 30.

Rnd 14: *Sc 1, sc2tog; rep from * 9 more times. (20 sts)

Rnd 15: Sc 20.

Rnd 16: *Sc 3, sc2tog; rep from * 3 more times. (16 sts)

Rnd 17: Sc 16.

Rnd 18: *Sc 2, sc2tog; rep from * 3 more times. (12 sts)

Rnd 19: Sc 12.

Stuff body.

Rnd 20: *Sc 1, sc2tog; rep from * 3 more times. (8 sts)

Rnd 21: Sc 8.

Rnd 22: *Sc 2, sc2tog; rep from * 1 more time. (6 sts)

Fasten off, leaving a long tail. If you're not using plastic eyes, close 6-st hole and weave in end.

FLIPPER

Make 2.

Using gray yarn, make a 6-st adjustable ring.

Rnd 1: Sc 3, sc 2 in next sc, sc 3 in next sc, sc 2 in next sc. (10 sts)

Rnd 2: Sc 3, *sc 2 in next sc; rep from * 6 more times. (17 sts)

Rnds 3–5: Sc 17.

Rnd 6: Sc2tog, *sc 1, sc2tog; rep from * 4 more times. (11 sts)

Rnd 7: Sc 1, *sc 3, sc2tog; rep from * 1 more time. (9 sts)

Rnd 8: Sc 9.

Rnd 9: Sc 7, sc2tog. (8 sts)

Rnd 10: Sc2tog 4 times. (4 sts)

Fasten off. Flatten seam and sew closed, leaving a long tail.

MUZZLE

Using gray yarn, make an 8-st adjustable ring.

Rnd 1: Sc 2 in each sc. (16 sts)

Rnd 2: *Sc 1, sc 2 in next sc; rep from * 7 more times. (24 sts)

Rnd 3: Sc 24.

Rnd 4: *Sc 1, sc2tog; rep from * 7 more times. (16 sts)

Fasten off, leaving a long tail.

ASSEMBLY

1 Using gray yarn, sew open edge of muzzle to larger, rounder front end of body. Stuff lightly before closing seam.

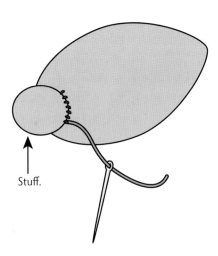

Stuff.

2 Using black yarn, apply French knots (page 18) directly above muzzle, about 6 sts apart. For non-bath toys, attach plastic eyes or sew on felt circles. With black yarn, embroider eyebrows above eyes using a lazy daisy st (page 18). Close 6-st hole and weave in

end. Using black yarn, make a lip cleft by looping a long st (page 19) from bottom of chin up through middle of muzzle and back out at chin again, pulling tightly to form 2 cheeks, rep 2 or 3 times. Add a short st for nostrils to front of each cheek above cleft.

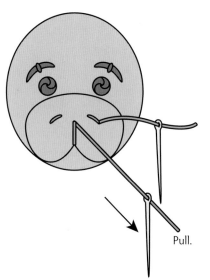

Pull.

3 Attach flippers to sides of body. Flatten tail and attach to back of body.

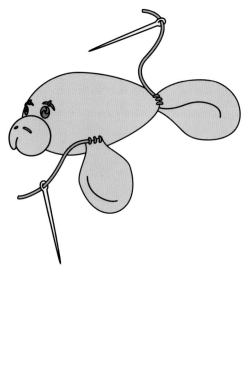

Sea Otter

This little sea otter is all set to chow down on a yummy clam lunch while floating around in your tub. If your sea otter is not destined for the bath, you could also make him some felt fish to play with.

Skill Level: Easy ◐■◻◻   **Finished Size:** Approx 7" long and 3" tall

MATERIALS

- Worsted-weight yarn in brown (approx 100 yds)
- Worsted-weight yarn in cream (approx 40 yds)
- Worsted-weight yarn in black (approx 5 yds)
- Worsted-weight yarn in gray (approx 10 yds)
- Size F-5 (3.75 mm) crochet hook
- Tapestry needle
- Sponge stuffing for bath toy
- For non-bath toy: 8 mm or 9 mm black plastic eyes with safety backings and toy stuffing
- Stitch markers to indicate beginning of rnds (optional)

HEAD

Using cream yarn, make an 8-st adjustable ring (page 14).

Rnd 1: Sc 2 in each sc around. (16 sts)

Rnd 2: *Sc 3, sc 2 in next sc; rep from * 3 more times. (20 sts)

Rnd 3: *Sc 1, sc 2 in next sc; rep from * 9 more times. (30 sts)

Rnd 4: *Sc 4, sc 2 in next sc; rep from * 5 more times. (36 sts)

Rnds 5–9: Sc 36.

Rnd 10: *Sc 4, sc2tog; rep from * 5 more times. (30 sts)

Rnd 11: *Sc 1, sc2tog; rep from * 9 more times. (20 sts)

Rnd 12: *Sc 3, sc2tog; rep from * 3 more times. (16 sts)

Rnd 13: Sc2tog 8 times. (8 sts)

Stuff head.

Rnd 14: *Sc 2, sc2tog; rep from * 1 more time. (6 sts)

Fasten off, leaving a long tail.

EAR

Make 2.

Using brown yarn, make a 4-st adjustable ring.

Fasten off, leaving a long tail.

BODY

Using brown yarn, make an 8-st adjustable ring.

Rnd 1: Sc 2 in each sc around. (16 sts)

Rnd 2: *Sc 3, sc 2 in next sc; rep from * 3 more times. (20 sts)

Rnd 3: *Sc 1, sc 2 in next sc; rep from * 9 more times. (30 sts)

Rnds 4–8: Sc 30.

Rnd 9: *Sc 1, sc2tog; rep from * 9 more times. (20 sts)

Rnd 10: Sc 20.

Rnd 11: *Sc 3, sc2tog; rep from * 3 more times. (16 sts)

Rnd 12: Sc 16.

Rnd 13: *Sc 2, sc2tog; rep from * 3 more times. (12 sts)

Rnd 14: Sc 12.

Rnd 15: *Sc 1, sc2tog; rep from * 3 more times. (8 sts)

Rnds 16 and 17: Sc 8.

Stuff body and tail.

Rnd 18: *Sc 2, sc2tog; rep from * 1 more time. (6 sts)

Rnds 19 and 20: Sc 6.

Finish stuffing tail.

Rnd 21: *Sc 1, sc2tog; rep from * 1 more time. (4 sts)

Fasten off, leaving a long tail. Close 4-st hole and weave in end.

PAW

Make 4.

Using brown yarn, make a 6-st adjustable ring.

Rnd 1: Sc 3, sc 2 in next sc, sc 3 in next sc, sc 2 in next sc. (10 sts)

Rnd 2: Sc 3, *sc 2 in next sc; rep from * 6 more times. (17 sts)

Rnds 3–5: Sc 17.

Rnd 6: Sc2tog, *sc 1, sc2tog; rep from * 4 more times. (11 sts)

Rnd 7: Sc 1, *sc 3, sc2tog; rep from * 1 more time. (9 sts)

Rnd 8: Sc 9.

Rnd 9: *Sc 1, sc2tog; rep from * 2 more times. (6 sts)

Fasten off. Flatten seam and sew closed, leaving a long yarn tail.

MUZZLE

Using cream yarn, make an 8-st adjustable ring.

Rnd 1: Sc 2 in each sc around. (16 sts)

Rnd 2: *Sc 1, sc 2 in next st; rep from * 7 more times. (24 sts)

Rnd 3: Sc 24.

Rnd 4: *Sc 1, sc2tog; rep from * 7 more times. (16 sts)

Sl st in next sc to fasten off, leaving a long tail.

CLAM SHELL

Make 2.

Using gray yarn, make a 6-st adjustable ring. Ch 1 and turn.

Row 1: Sk first ch, sc 6, ch 1 and turn. (6 sts)

Row 2: Sk first ch, sc 6 and fasten off, leaving a long tail. (6 sts)

With WS tog, whipstitch shells tog along straight edge at bottom.

ASSEMBLY

1 Using cream yarn, sew open edge of muzzle to front of head. Stuff lightly before closing seam. Using black yarn, apply French knots (page 18) directly above muzzle, about 6 sts apart. For non-bath toys, attach plastic eyes or sew on felt circles. With black yarn, embroider eyebrows above eyes using lazy daisy st (page 18). Using leftover yarn tails, attach ears at sides of head.

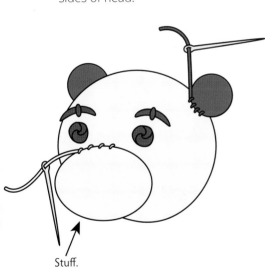

Stuff.

2 Using black yarn, make lip cleft by looping a long st (page 19) from bottom of chin up through middle of muzzle and back out at chin again, pulling tightly to form 2 cheeks; rep 2 or 3 times. Using black yarn, apply nose at top of lip cleft (see "Satin-Stitch Nose"

below). Make 3 short sts on side of each cheek for whiskers.

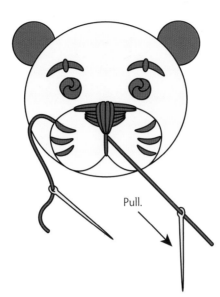

Pull.

3 Using cream yarn, attach head to body angling head to work with curvature of body and back. Using brown yarn, attach paws at shoulders and hips. For front paws, check to make sure paws can meet in middle before sewing in place if you want your otter to hold a clam.

4 Using black yarn and a tapestry needle, embroider 4 long perpendicular sts at end of each paw to separate toes. Place clam between front paws and sew in place.

Satin-Stitch Nose

With black yarn and a tapestry needle, sew 2 stitches from A to B, 4 stitches from C to D, and 4 stitches from E to F, taking care to keep the yarn and stitches very close together.

Lobster

Red lobsters are a fairly common sight after they take a dip in a boiling pot of water. But there are other color options as well! The most common coloring is dark turquoise or brown, but one in 2 million lobsters are blue, one in 30 million are yellow, and one in 100 million are albino. One in 50 million lobsters are split evenly down the middle— orange on one side, blue on the other.

Skill Level: Easy ◼◼◻◻   **Finished Size:** Approx 7" long and 8" wide

MATERIALS

Worsted-weight yarn in red (125 yds)
Worsted-weight yarn in black (10 yds)
Size F-5 (3.75 mm) crochet hook
Tapestry needle
Sponge stuffing for bath toy
For non-bath toy: 8 mm or 9 mm black plastic eyes with safety backings and toy stuffing
Stitch markers to indicate beginning of rnds (optional)

BODY

Using red yarn, make a 4-st adjustable ring (page 14).

Rnd 1: Sc 2 in each st around. (8 sts)

Rnd 2: *Sc 1, sc 2 in next st; rep from * 3 more times. (12 sts)

Rnd 3: *Sc 5, sc 2 in next st; rep from * 1 more time. (14 sts)

Rnd 4: *Sc 6, sc 2 in next st; rep from * 1 more time. (16 sts)

Rnd 5: *Sc 3, sc 2 in next st; rep from * 3 more times. (20 sts)

Rnd 6: *Sc 1, sc 2 in next st; rep from * 9 more times. (30 sts)

Rnd 7: Sc2tog 15 times. (15 sts)

Rnd 8: In fl, sc 2 in each st around. (30 sts)

Rnd 9: *Sc 3, sc2tog; rep from * 5 more times. (24 sts)

Rnd 10: Sc 24.

Rnd 11: *Sc 4, sc2tog; rep from * 3 more times. (20 sts)

Rnds 12–14: Sc 20.

Rnd 15: Sc2tog 10 times. (10 sts)

Rnd 16: In fl, sc 2 in each st around. (20 sts)

Rnd 17: Sc2tog 10 times. (10 sts)

Rnd 18: In fl, sc 2 in each st around. (20 sts)

Rnd 19: Sc2tog 10 times. (10 sts)

Rnd 20: In fl, sc 2 in each st around. (20 sts)

Rnd 21: Sc2tog 10 times. (10 sts)
Stuff body.

Rnd 22: *Sc 3, sc2tog; rep from * 1 more time. (8 sts)
Fasten off, leaving a long tail.

TAIL

Using red yarn, loosely ch 9.

Row 1: Starting in 2nd ch from hook and working in back ridge lps; *(hdc 1, dc 1, tr 1, dc 1, hdc 1) in next ch, sl st 1; rep from * 3 more times. Ch 1 and turn. (24 sts)

Row 2: Sk first ch, *sl st 2, hdc 4 in next st, sl st 3; rep from * 3 more times.
Fasten off, leaving a long tail.

LEG

Make 8.
Using red yarn, make a 4-st adjustable ring.

Rnd 1: In bl, sc 4.

Rnds 2–5: Sc 4.

Rnd 6: In fl, sc 2 in each sc around. (8 sts)

Rnd 7: Sc2tog 4 times. (4 sts)

Rnds 8–10: Sc 4.
Fasten off, leaving a long tail. Thread yarn tail up through leg to leg's base at rnd 1.

LARGE CLAW

Make 2.
Using red yarn, make a 6-st adjustable ring.

Rnd 1: In bl, sc 6.

Rnds 2 and 3: Sc 6.

Rnd 4: In fl, sc 2 in each sc around. (12 sts)

Rnd 5: Sc2tog 6 times. (6 sts)

Rnds 6 and 7: Sc 6.

Rnd 8: In fl, sc 2 in each sc around. (12 sts)

Rnd 9: Sc 12.

Rnd 10: *Sc 2, sc 2 in next sc; rep from * 3 more times. (16 sts)

Rnds 11 and 12: Sl st 4, hdc 8, sl st 4. (16 sts)

Rnd 13: Sl st 4, hdc 2, dc 4, hdc 2, sl st 4. (16 sts)

Rnd 14: Sc2tog 8 times. (8 sts)
Stuff claw.

Rnd 15: Sc2tog 4 times. (4 sts)
Fasten off. Close 4-st hole, leaving a long tail.

SMALL CLAW

Make 2.

Using red yarn, loosely ch 4.

Rnd 1: Starting in 2nd ch from hook and working in back ridge lps; sc 1, hdc 1, dc 2 in next ch. Rotate work. Starting in next ch and working in front lps; hdc 1, sc 1 in next ch. (6 sts)

Rnd 2: Sc 2 in each st around. (12 sts)

Fasten off, leaving a long tail.

ANTENNA

Using red yarn, loosely ch 24. Starting in 2nd ch from hook and working in back ridge lps, sl st 23. Fasten off, weave in end.

ASSEMBLY

❶ Fold antenna in half to locate midpoint. Using a small piece of red yarn, attach midpoint of antenna to front of head. Attach 4 legs and 1 large claw to each side of body between head and tail.

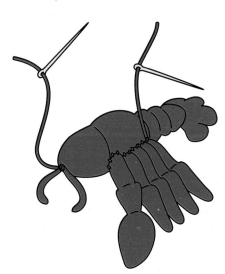

❷ Press your finger into the small claws so they form a concave

shape with RS facing out. Using red yarn, sew small claws to inside edge at base of the largest portion of large claws to create the pinchers.

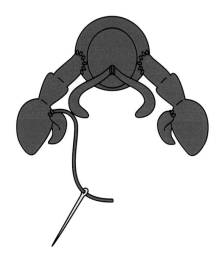

❸ Using black yarn, apply French knots (page 18) to sides of head. For non-bath toys, attach plastic eyes or sew on felt circles (you may need to remove some stuffing temporarily to make installing safety eyes easier). With black yarn, embroider eyebrows above eyes using lazy daisy st (page 18). Close 8-st hole and weave in end.

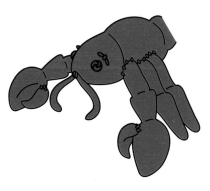

❹ Attach tail to back end of lobster.

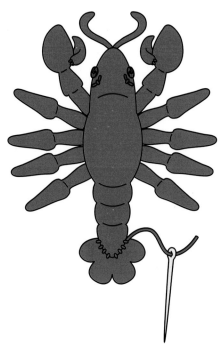

Blue Crab

One summer, a small group of friends and I took a boat out on the Long Island Sound to catch blue crabs. All we needed were a few wire coat hangers tied with rope and some chicken wings. The chicken wings were threaded onto the hangers and tossed into the water. The crabs would grab onto the chicken wings and we would simply lift them up onto the boat. Of course, if you don't have any chicken wings handy, you can always whip up a few crabs with this pattern and some extra skeins of yarn.

Skill Level: Easy ■■□□ **Finished Size:** Approx 5" long and 9" wide

MATERIALS

Worsted-weight yarn in taupe (approx 50 yds)

Worsted-weight yarn in cream (approx 50 yds)

Worsted-weight yarn in light blue (approx 50 yds)

Worsted-weight yarn in red (approx 10 yds)

Worsted-weight yarn in black (approx 5 yds)

Size F-5 (3.75 mm) crochet hook

Tapestry needle

Sponge stuffing for bath toys

For non-bath toys: 8 mm or 9 mm black plastic eyes with safety backings and toy stuffing

Stitch markers to indicate beginning of rnds (optional)

SHELL

Make 1 taupe and 1 cream.

Loosely ch 6.

Rnd 1: Starting in 2nd ch from hook and working in back ridge lps, sc 4, sc 5 in back ridge lp of next ch. Rotate work. Starting in next ch and working in front lps, sc 3, sc 4 in next ch. (16 sts)

Rnd 2: Sc 1, hdc 2 in next sc, dc 3 in next sc, hdc 2 in next sc, sc 2, hdc 3 in next sc, sc 7, hdc 3 in next sc, sc 1. (24 sts)

Rnd 3: Sc 2, hdc 2, hdc 2 in next st, hdc 2, sc 2, hdc 2, dc 3 in next st, hdc 2, dc 3 in next st, sl st 3, dc 3 in next st, hdc 2, dc 3 in next st, hdc 2. (33 sts)

Rnd 4: Sc 13, hdc 3 in next st, sc 4, hdc 2 in next st, sc 1, sl st 3, sc 1, hdc 2 in next st, sc 4, hdc 3 in next st, sc 3. (39 sts)

Rnd 5: Sc 39.

Rnd 6: In bl, *sl st 1, sc 3 in next st, sl st 1; rep from * 6 more times. In both lps, sl st 9. In bl, **sl st 1, sc 3 in next st, sl st 1; rep from ** 2 more times. (50 sts)

Fasten off, leaving a long tail.

EYESTALK

Make 2.

Using taupe yarn, make a 4-st adjustable ring (page 14).

Rnd 1: Sc 2 in each sc around. (8 sts)

Rnd 2: *Sc 1, sc 2 in next st; rep from * 3 more times. (12 sts)

Rnd 3: Sc2tog 6 times. (6 sts)

Add plastic eyes now if desired.

Rnd 4: *Sc 1, sc2tog; rep from * 1 more time. (4 sts)

Rnds 5 and 6: Sc 4.

Fasten off, leaving a long tail.

LEG

Make 8.

Using light-blue yarn, make a 4-st adjustable ring.

Rnd 1: In bl, sc 4.

Rnds 2–6: Sc 4.

Rnd 7: In fl, sc 2 in each st around. (8 sts)

Rnd 8: Sc2tog 4 times. (4 sts)

Rnds 9–11: Sc 4.

Fasten off, leaving a long tail. Thread yarn tail up through leg to leg's base at rnd 1.

LARGE CLAW

Make 2.

Using light-blue yarn, make a 6-st adjustable ring.

Rnd 1: In bl, sc 6.

Rnds 2–5: Sc 6.

Rnd 6: In fl, sc 2 in each sc around. (12 sts)

Rnd 7: Sc2tog 6 times. (6 sts)

Rnd 8: *Sc 1, sc2tog; rep from * 1 more time. (4 sts)

Rnd 9: Sc 4.

Rnd 10: In fl, sc 2 in each sc around. (8 sts)

Switch to red yarn.

Rnd 11: In bl, sc 8.

Rnds 12 and 13: Sc 8.

Rnd 14: Sl st 2, hdc 1, dc 2, hdc 1, sl st 2. (8 sts)

Stuff claw.

Rnd 15: Sc2tog, hdc 1, dc 2, hdc 1, sc2tog. (6 sts)

Fasten off. Close 6-st hole and weave in end.

SMALL CLAW

Make 2.

Using red yarn, loosely ch 6.

Starting in 2nd ch from hook and working in back ridge lps, sc 2, hdc 2, dc 2 in next ch. Rotate work. Starting in next ch and working in front lps, hdc 2, sc 2 in next ch.

Fasten off, leaving a long tail.

ASSEMBLY

❶ Using black yarn, apply French knots (page 18) to front of each eyestalk. For non-bath toys, sew on felt circles. For plastic eyes, refer to "Eyestalk" (page 57) and the patt on when to install them. With black yarn, embroider eyebrows above eyes using lazy daisy st (page 18).

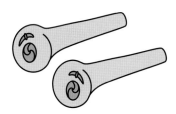

❷ With WS of cream shell facing up, position legs, claws, and eyestalks around edge of shell with about 2 rnds of overlap. Using cream yarn and running stitch

(page 19), sew around inside perimeter of shell to attach pieces to shell.

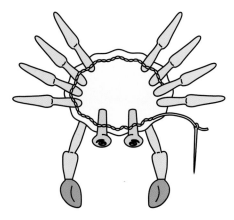

❸ Place taupe shell over cream-colored shell with RS facing up, sandwiching legs, claws, and eyestalks between two edges. Hold shells tog using safety pins or slip rings. Using taupe yarn and tapestry needle, sew running stitch or backstitch (page 18) through rnd 5 of both pieces leaving rnd 6 ruffled-edge free. Stuff before closing seam.

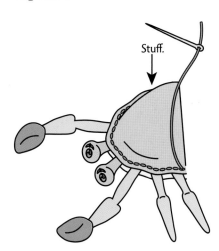

Stuff.

❹ Press your finger into the small claws so they form a concave shape with RS facing out. Using red yarn, sew small claws to inside edge at the base of red portion of large claws to create the pinchers.

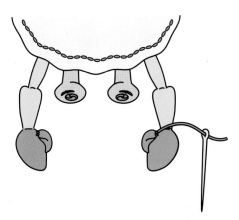

Swordfish

In the wild, swordfish have been reported to hit speeds of 60 miles (97 kilometers) per hour while hunting for food. With its skinny upper jaw and dorsal fin, this fish is built to cut through the water. Making a swordfish out of yarn will probably slow it down just a bit, making it much easier to catch in your tub!

Skill Level: Intermediate ■■■□   **Finished Size:** Approx 9" long and 4" tall

MATERIALS

Worsted-weight yarn in blue (approx 100 yds)
Worsted-weight yarn in black (approx 5 yds)
Size F-5 (3.75 mm) crochet hook
Tapestry needle
Marking pins
8" x 8" square of white terry cloth for bath toy or felt for non-bath toy
Sewing needle and white thread
Sponge stuffing for bath toy
For non-bath toy: 8 mm or 9 mm black plastic eyes with safety backings and toy stuffing
Stitch markers to indicate beginning of rnds (optional)

BODY

Using blue yarn, make a 4-st adjustable ring (page 14).

Rnds 1–5: Sc 4.

Rnd 6: *Sc 1, sc 2 in next sc; rep from * 1 more time. (6 sts)

Rnds 7–9: Sc 6.

Rnd 10: *Sc 2, sc 2 in next sc; rep from * 1 more time. (8 sts)

Rnd 11: *Sc 3, sc 2 in next sc; rep from * 1 more time. (10 sts)

Rnd 12: *Sc 4, sc 2 in next sc; rep from * 1 more time. (12 sts)

Rnd 13: *Sc 5, sc 2 in next sc; rep from * 1 more time. (14 sts)

Rnd 14: *Sc 6, sc 2 in next sc; rep from * 1 more time. (16 sts)

Rnd 15: *Sc 3, sc 2 in next sc; rep from * 3 more times. (20 sts)

Rnd 16: *Sc 4, sc 2 in next sc; rep from * 3 more times. (24 sts)

Rnds 17–21: Sc 24.

Rnd 22: *Sc 4, sc2tog; rep from * 3 more times. (20 sts)

Rnd 23: Sc 20.

Rnd 24: *Sc 3, sc2tog; rep from * 3 more times. (16 sts)

Rnd 25: Sc 16.

Rnd 26: *Sc 2, sc2tog; rep from * 3 more times. (12 sts)

Rnd 27: Sc 12.

Stuff body.

Rnd 28: *Sc 1, sc2tog; rep from * 3 more times. (8 sts)

Rnd 29: Sc 8.

Fasten off, leaving a long tail. If you're not using plastic eyes, close 8-st hole and weave in end.

SIDE FIN AND TAIL

Make 4.

Using blue yarn, make a 5-st adjustable ring.

Rnd 1: Sc 2 in each sc around. (10 sts)

Rnd 2: *Sc 4, sc 2 in next sc; rep from * 1 more time. (12 sts)

Rnds 3 and 4: Sc 12.

Rnd 5: *Sc 1, sc2tog; rep from * 3 more times. (8 sts)

Rnd 6: Sc 8.

Rnd 7: *Sc 2, sc2tog; rep from * 1 more time. (6 sts)

Rnd 8: Sc2tog 3 times. (3 sts)

Fasten off, leaving a long tail.

SMALL BELLY FIN

Using blue yarn, make a 4-st adjustable ring.

Rnd 1: *Sc 1, sc 2 in next sc; rep from * 1 more time. (6 sts)

Rnd 2: Sc 6.

Fasten off, leaving a long tail.

DORSAL FIN

Using blue yarn, make a 4-st adjustable ring.

Rnd 1: Sc 4.

Rnd 2: *Sc 1, sc 2 in next sc; rep from * 1 more time. (6 sts)

Rnd 3: Sc 6.

Rnd 4: *Sc 2, sc 2 in next sc; rep from * 1 more time. (8 sts)

Rnd 5: *Sc 3, sc 2 in next sc; rep from * 1 more time. (10 sts)

Rnd 6: Sc 10.

Rnd 7: *Sc 4, sc 2 in next sc; rep from * 1 more time. (12 sts)

Rnd 8: Sc 12.

Fasten off, leaving a long tail.

ASSEMBLY

1 Using pattern on page 87, cut 1 belly patch out of terry cloth or felt. Refer to page 21 for tips on how to prepare terry cloth for appliqué. For felt patch, sew dart tog where indicated before attaching patch to toy. Using illustration for reference, secure patch to bottom half of body using pins to ensure everything is even before sewing in place using a needle and thread and either running st (page 19) for felt, or appliqué stitch (page 19) for terry cloth.

2 Using tapestry needle and yarn, attach rounder portion of side fins to middle of body on each side, while taking care to sew through both belly patch and crocheted surface of toy. Flatten and attach dorsal fin to back of body directly above side fins. Attach belly fin to belly of body between side fins and the back of the toy.

3 Using black yarn, apply French knots (page 18) to sides of head. For non-bath toys, sew on felt circles or attach plastic eyes by making a hole in fabric patch using a tapestry needle first, before inserting the safety eye post. (You may need to remove some stuffing temporarily to make installing the safety eyes easier.) With black yarn, embroider eyebrows above eyes using lazy daisy st (page 18). Apply 2 or 3 short sts behind each eye for gills. Close 8-st hole and weave in end. Position tail fins so they're stacked vertically with their flat sides facing you when viewed in profile and their pointy ends pointing away from body. Using tapestry needle and blue yarn, attach larger, rounder portion of tail fins to end of swordfish body.

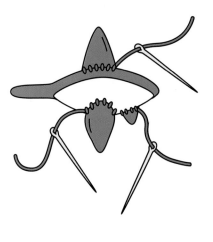

Terry cloth

Dolphin

Dolphins are very social and friendly animals, so I recommend making at least a few to keep each other company. After all, who wouldn't love a whole pod of dolphins doing tricks for them in the bathtub!

Skill Level: Intermediate ⬛⬛⬛⬜ **Finished Size:** Approx 7" long and 4" tall

MATERIALS

Worsted-weight yarn in light blue (approx 100 yds)
Worsted-weight yarn in black (approx 5 yds)
Size F-5 (3.75 mm) crochet hook
Tapestry needle
8" x 8" square of white terry cloth for bath toy or felt for non-bath toy
Sewing needle and white thread
Sponge stuffing for bath toy
For non-bath toy: 8 mm or 9 mm black plastic eyes with safety backings and toy stuffing
Straight pins
Stitch markers to indicate beginning of rnds (optional)

BODY

Using light-blue yarn, make a 6-st adjustable ring (page 14).

Rnd 1: Sc 6.
Rnd 2: Sc 5, sc 2 in next sc. (7 sts)
Rnd 3: Sc 6, sc 2 in next sc. (8 sts)
Rnd 4: Sc 7, sc 2 in next sc. (9 sts)
Rnd 5: *Sc 2, sc 2 in next sc; rep from * 2 more times. (12 sts)
Rnd 6: *Sc 2, sc 2 in next sc; rep from * 3 more times. (16 sts)
Rnd 7: *Sc 3, sc 2 in next sc; rep from * 3 more times. (20 sts)
Rnd 8: *Sc 1, sc 2 in next sc; rep from * 9 more times. (30 sts)
Rnds 9–11: Sc 30.

Rnd 12: *Sc 4, sc 2 in next sc; rep from * 5 more times. (36 sts)
Rnds 13–15: Sc 36.
Rnd 16: *Sc 4, sc2tog; rep from * 5 more times. (30 sts)
Rnds 17 and 18: Sc 30.
Rnd 19: *Sc 1, sc2tog; rep from * 9 more times. (20 sts)
Rnd 20: Sc 20.
Rnd 21: *Sc 3, sc2tog; rep from * 3 more times. (16 sts)
Rnd 22: Sc 16.
Rnd 23: *Sc2, sc2tog; rep from * 3 more times. (12 sts)
Rnd 24: Sc 12.
Stuff body.
Rnd 25: *Sc 1, sc2tog; rep from * 3 more times. (8 sts)
Rnd 26: Sc 8.
Fasten off, leaving a long tail. If you're not using plastic eyes, close 8-st hole and weave in end.

FLIPPER

Make 2.

Using light-blue yarn, make a 5-st adjustable ring.

Rnd 1: Sc 2 in each sc around. (10 sts)
Rnd 2: *Sc 4, sc 2 in next sc; rep from * 1 more time. (12 sts)
Rnds 3 and 4: Sc 12.
Rnd 5: *Sc 1, sc2tog; rep from * 3 more times. (8 sts)
Rnd 6: Sc 8.
Rnd 7: *Sc 2, sc2tog; rep from * 1 more time. (6 sts)
Rnd 8: Sc2tog 3 times. (3 sts)
Fasten off, leaving a long tail.

TAIL FIN

Make 2.

Using light-blue yarn, make a 6-st adjustable ring.

Rnd 1: Sc 3, sc 2 in next sc, sc 3 in next sc, sc 2 in next sc. (10 sts)
Rnd 2: Sc 3, *sc 2 in next sc; rep from * 6 more times. (17 sts)
Rnds 3–5: Sc 17.
Rnd 6: Sc2tog, *sc 1, sc2tog; rep from * 4 more times. (11 sts)
Rnd 7: Sc 1, *sc 3, sc2tog; rep from * 1 more time. (9 sts)
Rnd 8: Sc 9.
Rnd 9: *Sc 1, sc2tog; rep from * 2 more times. (6 sts)
Rnd 10: *Sc 1, sc2tog; rep from * 1 more time. (4 sts)
Fasten off, leaving a long tail.

DORSAL FIN

Using light-blue yarn, make a 4-st adjustable ring.

Rnd 1: Sc 4.

Rnd 2: Sc 2 in each sc around. (8 sts)

Rnd 3: Sc 7, sc 2 in next sc. (9 sts)

Rnd 4: Sc 9.

Rnd 5: Sc 2 in next sc, sc 4, sc 2 in next sc, sc 3. (11 sts)

Fasten off, leaving a long tail.

ASSEMBLY

1 Using pattern on page 90, cut 1 belly patch out of terry cloth or felt. Refer to page 21 for tips on how to prepare terry cloth for appliqué. For felt patch, sew dart before attaching patch to toy. Using illustration for reference, secure patch to bottom half of body using pins to ensure everything is even before sewing in place. Sew tog using either running stitch (page 19) for felt, or appliqué stitch (page 19) for terry cloth.

2 Using light-blue yarn, attach rounder portion of flippers to middle of body on each side directly above belly patch. Flatten and attach dorsal fin to back of body directly above the flippers. Using black yarn, apply French knots (page 18) to sides of head about 2 rnds in front of flippers and 1 st above belly patch. For non-bath toys, attach plastic eyes or sew on felt circles (you may need to remove some stuffing temporarily to make installing safety eyes easier). With black yarn, embroider eyebrows above eyes using lazy daisy st (page 18). Close 8-st hole and weave in end. Embroider an X at top of head in front of dorsal fin, for blowhole.

3 Position tail fins so they line up next to each other with their flat sides facing up. Attach larger, rounder portion of tail fins to end of dolphin body using light-blue yarn.

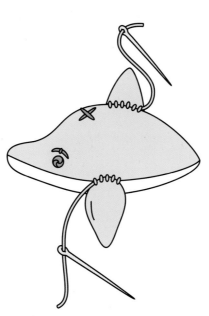

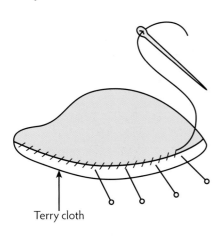

Terry cloth

Narwhal

Sometimes called the unicorn of the sea, the narwhal's tusk is actually a really long tooth. Some tusks can grow over eight feet long! Narwhals live mostly in cold, Arctic coastal waters. If you happen to invite a small pod of Narwhals into your tub, I'm sure they will be willing to make do with slightly warmer water.

Skill Level: Intermediate ■■■□ **Finished Size:** Approx 10" long and 3" tall

MATERIALS

Worsted-weight yarn in charcoal (120 yds)
Worsted-weight yarn in light gray (10 yds)
Size F-5 (3.75 mm) crochet hook
Tapestry needle
8" x 8" square of white terry cloth for bath toy or felt for non-bath toy
Sewing needle and white thread
Sponge stuffing for bath toy
For non-bath toy: 8 mm or 9 mm black plastic eyes with safety backings and toy stuffing
Straight pins
Stitch markers to indicate beginning of rnds (optional)

BODY

Using charcoal yarn, make an 8-st adjustable ring (page 14).

Rnd 1: Sc 2 in each sc around. (16 sts)

Rnd 2: *Sc 1, sc 2 in next st; rep from * 7 more times. (24 sts)

Rnd 3: Sc 24.

Rnd 4: *Sc 3, sc 2 in next st; rep from * 5 more times. (30 sts)

Rnds 5 and 6: Sc 30.

Rnd 7: *Sc 3, sc2tog; rep from * 5 more times. (24 sts)

Rnds 8 and 9: Sc 24.

Rnd 10: *Sc 3, sc 2 in next sc; rep from * 5 more times. (30 sts)

Rnd 11: *Sc 4, sc 2 in next sc; rep from * 5 more times. (36 sts)

Rnds 12–14: Sc 36.

Rnd 15: *Sc 4 sc2tog; rep from * 5 more times. (30 sts)

Rnds 16 and 17: Sc 30.

Rnd 18: *Sc 3, sc2tog; rep from * 5 more times. (24 sts)

Rnd 19: Sc 24.

Rnd 20: *Sc 4, sc2tog; rep from * 3 more times. (20 sts)

Rnd 21: Sc 20.

Rnd 22: *Sc 3, sc2tog; rep from * 3 more times. (16 sts)

Rnd 23: Sc 16.

Rnd 24: *Sc 2, sc2tog; rep from * 3 more times. (12 sts)

Rnd 25: Sc 12.

Stuff body.

Rnd 26: *Sc 1, sc2tog; rep from * 3 more times. (8 sts)

Rnd 27: Sc 8.

Fasten off, leaving a long tail. If you're not using plastic eyes, close 8-st hole and weave in end.

FLIPPER

Make 2.

Using charcoal yarn, make a 6-st adjustable ring.

Rnd 1: Sc 3, sc 2 in next sc, sc 3 in next sc, sc 2 in next sc. (10 sts)

Rnd 2: Sc 3, *sc 2 in next sc; rep from * 6 more times. (17 sts)

Rnds 3–5: Sc 17.

Rnd 6: Sc2tog, *sc 1, sc2tog; rep from * 4 more times. (11 sts)

Rnd 7: Sc 1, *sc 3, sc2tog; rep from * 1 more time. (9 sts)

Rnd 8: Sc 9.

Rnd 9: *Sc 1, sc2tog; rep from * 2 more times. (6 sts)

Fasten off, leaving a long tail.

TAIL FIN

Make 2.

Using charcoal yarn, make a 6-st adjustable ring.

Rnd 1: Sc 3, sc 2 in next sc, sc 3 in next sc, sc 2 in next sc. (10 sts)

Rnd 2: Sc 3, *sc 2 in next sc; rep from * 6 more times. (17 sts)

Rnds 3–5: Sc 17.

Rnd 6: Sc2tog, *sc 1, sc2tog; rep from * 4 more times. (11 sts)

Rnd 7: Sc 1, *sc 3, sc2tog; rep from * 1 more time. (9 sts)

Rnd 8: Sc 9.

Rnd 9: *Sc 1, sc2tog; rep from * 2 more times. (6 sts)

Rnd 10: *Sc 1, sc2tog; rep from * 1 more time. (4 sts)

Fasten off, leaving a long tail.

TUSK

Using light-gray yarn, make an 8-st adjustable ring.

Rnds 1 and 2: In bl, sc 8.

Rnd 3: In bl, sc 6, sc2tog. (7 sts)

Rnd 4: In bl, sc 5, sc2tog. (6 sts)
Rnd 5: In bl, sc 4, sc2tog. (5 sts)
Rnd 6: In bl, sc 3, sc2tog. (4 sts)
Fasten off, leaving a long tail.

ASSEMBLY

❶ Using pattern on page 90, cut 1 belly patch out of terry cloth or felt. Refer to page 21 for tips on how to prepare terry cloth for appliqué. For felt patch, sew dart before attaching patch to toy. Using the illustration for reference, secure patch to bottom half of body with pins to ensure everything is even before sewing in place. Using a needle and thread and either running stitch (page 19) for felt, or appliqué stitch (page 19) for terry cloth, sew patch to body.

❷ Using black yarn, attach smaller end of flippers directly above narwhal belly patch a few rnds in front of the middle of body on each side. Using black yarn, apply French knots (page 18) to sides of head through belly patch taking care to leave enough room for eyebrows. For non-bath toys, sew on felt circles or attach plastic eyes by making a hole in belly patch using a tapestry needle before inserting the safety eye post. (You may need to remove some stuffing temporarily to make installing safety eyes easier.) With black yarn, embroider eyebrows above eyes using lazy daisy st (page 18). Close 8-st hole and weave in ends. Using light-gray yarn, embroider a small X on back where head meets body for blowhole.

❸ Using light-gary yarn, attach tusk to front of head. Position tail fins so they line up next to each other with their flat sides facing up. Attach larger, rounder portion of tail fins to end of narwhal body.

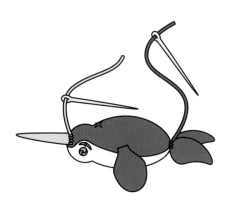

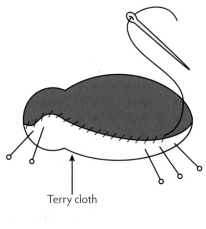

Terry cloth

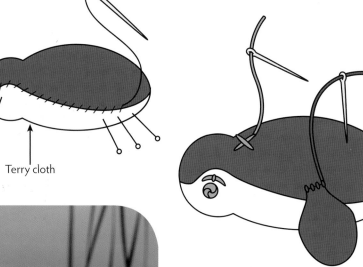

Blue Whale

The biggest animals on the earth to date, blue whales are really impressive. Their hearts can be as big as a small car, and their tails can rival the width of a small aircraft's wingspan. This pattern is a slightly scaled-down version, but if you'd like to make a bigger version using chunky yarn and a larger hook, make sure you scale up the belly patch on your printer or copier.

Skill Level: Intermediate ●■■□　　**Finished Size:** Approx 3" tall and 8" long

MATERIALS

Worsted-weight yarn in blue (approx 125 yds) (4)
Worsted-weight yarn in black (approx 5 yds)
Size F-5 (3.75 mm) crochet hook
9" x 9" square of white or light-blue terry cloth for bath toy, or felt for non-bath toy
Sewing needle and white or light blue thread
Sponge stuffing for bath toy
For non-bath toy: 8 mm or 9 mm black plastic eyes with safety backings and toy stuffing
Straight pins
Stitch markers to indicate beginning of rnds (optional)

BODY

Using blue yarn, make an 8-st adjustable ring (page 14).

Rnd 1: *Sc 1, sc 2 in next sc; rep from * 3 more times. (12 sts)

Rnd 2: *Sc 2, sc 2 in next sc; rep from * 3 more times. (16 sts)

Rnds 3 and 4: Sc 16.

Rnd 5: *Sc 7, sc 2 in next sc; rep from * 1 more time. (18 sts)

Rnds 6 and 7: Sc 18.

Rnd 8: *Sc 8, sc 2 in next sc; rep from * 1 more time. (20 sts)

Rnds 9 and 10: Sc 20.

Rnd 11: *Sc 4, sc 2 in next sc; rep from * 3 more times. (24 sts)

Rnd 12: Sc 24.

Rnd 13: *Sc 5, sc 2 in next sc; rep from * 3 more times. (28 sts)

Rnd 14: *Sc 6, sc 2 in next sc; rep from * 3 more times. (32 sts)

Rnds 15–18: Sc 32.

Rnd 19: *Sc 6, sc2tog; rep from * 3 more times. (28 sts)

Rnd 20: Sc 28.

Rnd 21: *Sc 5, sc2tog; rep from * 3 more times. (24 sts)

Rnd 22: Sc 24.

Rnd 23: *Sc 4, sc2tog; rep from * 3 more times. (20 sts)

Rnds 24 and 25: Sc 20.

Rnd 26: *Sc 3, sc2tog; rep from * 3 more times. (16 sts)

Rnds 27 and 28: Sc 16.

Rnd 29: *Sc 2, sc2tog; rep from * 3 more times. (12 sts)

Rnd 30: Sc 12.

Stuff body.

Rnd 31: *Sc 1, sc2tog; rep from * 3 more times. (8 sts)

Fasten off, leaving a long tail. If you're not using plastic eyes, close 8-st hole and weave in end.

FLIPPER

Make 2.

Using blue yarn, make a 6-st adjustable ring.

Rnd 1: Sc 3, sc 2 in next sc, sc 3 in next sc, sc 2 in next sc. (10 sts)

Rnd 2: Sc 3, *sc 2 in next sc; rep from * 6 more times. (17 sts)

Rnds 3–5: Sc 17.

Rnd 6: Sc2tog, *sc 1, sc2tog; rep from * 4 more times. (11 sts)

Rnd 7: Sc 1, *sc 3, sc2tog; rep from * 1 more time. (9 sts)

Rnd 8: Sc 9.

Rnd 9: *Sc 1, sc2tog; rep from * 2 more times. (6 sts)

Fasten off, leaving a long tail.

TAIL FIN

Make 2.

Using blue yarn, make a 6-st adjustable ring.

Rnd 1: Sc 3, sc 2 in next sc, sc 3 in next sc, sc 2 in next sc. (10 sts)

Rnd 2: Sc 3, *sc 2 in next sc; rep from * 6 more times. (17 sts)

Rnd 3–5: Sc 17.

Rnd 6: Sc2tog, *sc 1, sc2tog; rep from * 4 more times. (11 sts)

Rnd 7: Sc 1, *sc 3, sc2tog; rep from * 1 more time. (9 sts)

Rnd 8: Sc 9.

Rnd 9: *Sc 1, sc2tog; rep from * 2 more times. (6 sts)

Rnd 10: *Sc 1, sc2tog; rep from * 1 more time. (4 sts)

Fasten off, leaving a long tail.

DORSAL FIN

Using blue yarn, make a 4-st adjustable ring.

Rnd 1: *Sc 1, sc 2 in next sc; rep from * 1 more time. (6 sts)

Rnd 2: Sc 6.

Fasten off, leaving a long tail.

ASSEMBLY

1 Using pattern on page 89, cut 1 belly patch out of terry cloth or felt. Refer to page 21 for tips on how to prepare terry cloth for appliqué. For felt patch, sew dart before attaching patch to toy. Using the illustration for reference, secure patch to bottom half of body with pins to ensure everything is even before sewing in place. Using a needle and thread and either running st (page 19) for felt, or appliqué stitch (page 19) for terry cloth, sew patch to body.

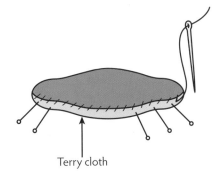

Terry cloth

2 Using blue yarn, backstitch (page 18) 3 long perpendicular lines along belly.

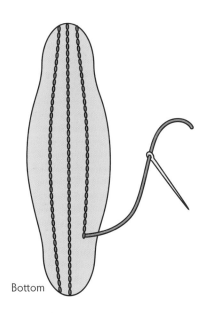

Bottom

3 Using blue yarn, attach the smaller end of flippers directly above belly patch a few rnds before the middle of body on each side. Attach dorsal fin to back between flippers and tail end of body. Using black yarn, apply French knots (page 18) to sides of head about 1 rnd in front of flippers and 1 st above belly patch. For non-bath toys, attach plastic eyes or sew on felt circles. (You may need to remove some stuffing temporarily to make installing safety eyes easier.) With black yarn,

embroider eyebrows above eyes using lazy daisy st (page 18). Close 8-st hole and weave in end. Using black yarn, embroider an X at top of head, above flippers for blowhole.

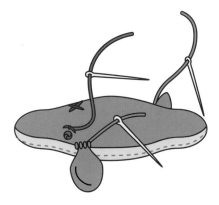

4 Using blue yarn, apply 9 to 11 French knots on front portion of snout to give the nose some texture. Position tail fins so they line up next to each other with their flat sides facing up. Attach larger, rounder portion of tail fins to end of blue-whale body.

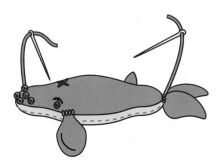

Orca

Orcas are some of the fastest marine mammals in the sea, reaching speeds up to 35 miles (56 kilometers) per hour. They are the largest members of the dolphin family and, like dolphins, are very social animals. If you happen to be making a non-bath toy orca, check out the tips on using all-black stuffing on page 8.

Skill Level: Intermediate ◼◼◼◻   **Finished Size:** Approx 8" long and 4" tall

MATERIALS

Worsted-weight yarn in black (120 yds)
Worsted-weight yarn in gray (5 yds)
Size F-5 (3.75 mm) crochet hook
8" x 8" square of white terry cloth for bath toy or felt for non-bath toy
Tapestry needle
Sewing needle and white thread
Sponge stuffing for bath toy
For non-bath toy: 8 mm or 9 mm black plastic eyes with safety backings and toy stuffing
Straight pins
Stitch markers to indicate beginning of rnds (optional)

BODY

Using black yarn, make an 8-st adjustable ring (page 14).

Rnd 1: *Sc 3, sc 2 in next sc; rep from * 1 more time. (10 sts)

Rnd 2: *Sc 4, sc 2 in next sc; rep from * 1 more time. (12 sts)

Rnd 3: Sc 12.

Rnd 4: *Sc 2, sc 2 in next st; rep from * 3 more times. (16 sts)

Rnd 5: *Sc 3, sc 2 in next st; rep from * 3 more times. (20 sts)

Rnd 6: *Sc 4, sc 2 in next st; rep from * 3 more times. (24 sts)

Rnd 7: *Sc 3, sc 2 in next st; rep from * 5 more times. (30 sts)

Rnds 8–10: Sc 30.

Rnd 11: *Sc 4, sc 2 in next sc; rep from * 5 more times. (36 sts)

Rnds 12–14: Sc 36.

Rnd 15: *Sc 4, sc2tog; rep from * 5 more times. (30 sts)

Rnds 16 and 17: Sc 30.

Rnd 18: *Sc 3, sc2tog; rep from * 5 more times. (24 sts)

Rnd 19: Sc 24.

Rnd 20: *Sc 4, sc2tog; rep from * 3 more times. (20 sts)

Rnds 21 and 22: Sc 20.

Rnd 23: *Sc 3, sc2tog; rep from * 3 more times. (16 sts)

Rnd 24: Sc 16.

Rnd 25: *Sc 2, sc2tog; rep from * 3 more times. (12 sts)

Rnd 26: Sc 12.

Stuff body.

Rnd 27: *Sc 1, sc2tog; rep from * 3 more times. (8 sts)

Rnd 28: Sc 8.

Fasten off, leaving a long tail. If you're not using plastic eyes, close 8-st hole and weave in end.

FLIPPER

Make 2.

Using black yarn, make a 6-st adjustable ring.

Rnd 1: Sc 3, sc 2 in next sc, sc 3 in next sc, sc 2 in next sc. (10 sts)

Rnd 2: Sc 3, *sc 2 in next sc; rep from * 6 more times. (17 sts)

Rnds 3–5: Sc 17.

Rnd 6: Sc2tog, *sc 1, sc2tog; rep from * 4 more times. (11 sts)

Rnd 7: Sc 1, *sc 3, sc2tog; rep from * 1 more time. (9 sts)

Rnd 8: Sc 9.

Rnd 9: *Sc 1, sc2tog; rep from * 2 more times. (6 sts)

Fasten off, leaving a long tail.

TAIL FIN

Make 2.

Using black yarn, make a 6-st adjustable ring.

Rnd 1: Sc 3, sc 2 in next sc, sc 3 in next sc, sc 2 in next sc. (10 sts)

Rnd 2: Sc 3, *sc 2 in next sc; rep from * 6 more times. (17 sts)

Rnds 3–5: Sc 17.

Rnd 6: Sc2tog, *sc 1, sc2tog; rep from * 4 more times. (11 sts)

Rnd 7: Sc 1, *sc 3, sc2tog; rep from * 1 more time. (9 sts)

Rnd 8: Sc 9.

Rnd 9: *Sc 1, sc2tog; rep from * 2 more times. (6 sts)

Rnd 10: *Sc 1, sc2tog; rep from * 1 more time. (4 sts)

Fasten off, leaving a long tail.

DORSAL FIN

Using black yarn, make a 4-st adjustable ring.

Rnd 1: Sc 4.

Rnd 2: *Sc 1, sc 2 in next sc; rep from * 1 more time. (6 sts)

Rnd 3: Sc 6.

Rnd 4: *Sc 2, sc 2 in next sc; rep from * 1 more time. (8 sts)

Rnd 5: Sc 2 in next sc, sc 7. (9 sts)

Rnd 6: Sc 9.

Rnd 7: Sc 2 in next sc, sc 4, sc 2 in next sc, sc 3. (11 sts)

Fasten off, leaving a long tail.

ASSEMBLY

❶ Using pattern on page 88, cut 1 belly patch out of terry cloth or felt. Refer to page 21 for tips on how to prepare terry cloth for appliqué. Using illustration for reference, secure belly patch to bottom half of body using pins to ensure everything is even before sewing in place. Using needle and thread and either running stitch (page 19) for felt, or appliqué stitch (page 19) for terry cloth, sew patch to body.

❷ Using black yarn, attach smaller end of flippers directly above belly patch, a few rnds before the middle of body on each side. Attach dorsal fin to back behind flippers. Using gray yarn, apply French knots (page 18) to sides of head about 7 rnds from front of nose. For non-bath toys, attach plastic eyes or sew on felt circles (you may need to remove some stuffing temporarily to make installing safety eyes easier). Close 8-st hole and weave in end. Using gray yarn, embroider an X at top of head 2 rnds in front of the dorsal fin for blowhole.

❸ Cut 2 eyespots (page 88) out of terry cloth or felt. Sew patches directly behind eyes. Position tail fins so they line up next to each other with their flat sides facing up. Attach larger, rounder portion of tail fins to end of orca body.

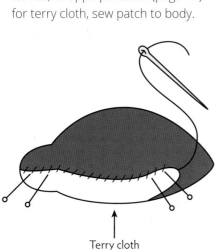

Terry cloth

Great White Shark and Hammerhead Shark

These sharks share the same body and fins, so it's up to you to customize them to your liking. All you need to do is choose whether or not to make a set of hammerhead eyes or an open jaw full of little white teeth. Smile!

Skill Level: Intermediate ⬛⬛⬛◻   **Finished Size:** Approx 7" long and 4" tall

MATERIALS

Worsted-weight yarn in gray or tan (approx 100 yds)

Worsted-weight yarn in black (approx 5 yds)

Optional for open jaw: worsted-weight yarn in red (approx 5 yds)

Optional for open jaw: worsted-weight yarn in white (approx 5 yds)

Size F-5 (3.75 mm) crochet hook

Tapestry needle

9" x 9" square of white terry cloth for bath toys or felt for non-bath toys

Sewing needle and white thread and (optional) red thread

Sponge stuffing for bath toys

For non-bath toys: 8 mm or 9 mm black plastic eyes with safety backings and toy stuffing

Straight pins

Stitch markers to indicate beginning of rnds (optional)

BODY

Using gray or tan yarn, make a 6-st adjustable ring (page 14).

Rnd 1: Sc 2 in each st around. (12 sts)

Rnd 2: Sc 12.

Rnd 3: *Sc 2, sc 2 in next sc; rep from * 3 more times. (16 sts)

Rnd 4: Sc 16.

Rnd 5: *Sc 3, sc 2 in next sc; rep from * 3 more times. (20 sts)

Rnds 6 and 7: Sc 20.

Rnd 8: *Sc 1, sc 2 in next sc; rep from * 9 more times. (30 sts)

Rnds 9–12: Sc 30.

Rnd 13: *Sc 4, sc 2 in next sc; rep from * 5 more times. (36 sts)

Rnd 14–16: Sc 36.

Rnd 17: *Sc 4, sc2tog; rep from * 5 more times. (30 sts)

Rnds 18 and 19: Sc 30.

Rnd 20: *Sc 1, sc2tog; rep from * 9 more times. (20 sts)

Rnds 21 and 22: Sc 20.

Rnd 23: *Sc 3, sc2tog; rep from * 3 more times. (16 sts)

Rnd 24: Sc 16.

Rnd 25: *Sc 2, sc2tog; rep from * 3 more times. (12 sts)

Rnd 26: Sc 12.

Stuff body.

Rnd 27: *Sc 1, sc2tog; rep from * 3 more times. (8 sts)

Rnd 28: Sc 8.

Fasten off, leaving a long tail. If you're not using plastic eyes, close 8-st hole and weave in end.

SIDE AND TAIL FIN

Make 4.

Using gray or tan yarn, make a 5-st adjustable ring.

Rnd 1: Sc 2 in each st around. (10 sts)

Rnd 2: *Sc 4, sc 2 in next sc; rep from * 1 more time. (12 sts)

Rnds 3 and 4: Sc 12.

Rnd 5: *Sc 1, sc2tog; rep from * 3 more times. (8 sts)

Rnd 6: Sc 8.

Rnd 7: *Sc 2, sc2tog; rep from * 1 more time. (6 sts)

Rnd 8: Sc2tog 3 times. (3 sts)

Fasten off, leaving a long tail.

SMALL FIN

Make 3.

Using gray or tan yarn, make a 4-st adjustable ring.

Rnd 1: *Sc 1, sc 2 in next sc; rep from * 1 more time. (6 sts)

Rnd 2: Sc 6.

Fasten off, leaving a long tail.

DORSAL FIN

Using gray or tan yarn, make a 4-st adjustable ring.

Rnd 1: Sc 4.

Rnd 2: *Sc 1, sc 2 in next sc; rep from * 1 more time. (6 sts)

Rnd 3: Sc 6.

Rnd 4: *Sc 2, sc 2 in next sc; rep from * 1 more time. (8 sts)

Rnd 5: *Sc 3, sc 2 in next sc; rep from * 1 more time. (10 sts)

Rnd 6: Sc 10.

Rnd 7: *Sc 4, sc 2 in next sc; rep from * 1 more time. (12 sts)

Rnd 8: Sc 12.

Fasten off, leaving a long tail.

HAMMERHEAD EYES

Using gray or tan yarn, make a 6-st adjustable ring.

Rnd 1: Sc 2 in each st around. (12 sts)

Rnd 2: Sc 12.

Rnd 3: Sc2tog 6 times. (6 sts)

For non-bath toys, install one plastic eye at the center of rnd 1 and then stuff lightly.

Rnds 4–13: Sc 6.

Rnd 14: Sc 2 in each sc around. (12 sts)

Rnd 15: Sc 12.

For non-bath toys, stuff lightly.

Rnd 16: Sc2tog 6 times. (6 sts)

Fasten off, leaving a long tail for sewing for bath toys.

For non-bath toys, place plastic safety eye backing onto eye post, but do not push backing down all the way. Slip backing and post into 6-st hole at the center of rnd 16. Using leftover yarn tail, proceed to cinch hole, then secure eye in place by pushing backing down onto eye post the rest of the way.

OPEN JAW (OPTIONAL)

Using red yarn, loosely ch 5.

Rnd 1: Starting in 2nd ch from hook and working in back ridge lps, sc 3, sc 6 in back ridge lps of next ch. Rotate work. Starting in next ch and working in front lps, sc 2, sc 5 in next ch. (16 sts)

Rnd 2: Sc 3, *sc 2 in next sc; rep from * 4 more times, sc 3, **sc 2 in next sc; rep from ** 4 more times. (26 sts)

Rnd 3: Sc 26.

Fasten off, leaving a long tail.

ASSEMBLY

❶ Using pattern on page 91, cut 1 belly patch out of terry cloth or felt. Refer to page 21 for tips on how to prepare terry cloth for appliqué. For felt patch, sew dart before attaching patch to toy. Using illustration for reference, secure patch to bottom half of body with pins to ensure everything is even before sewing in place. Using needle and thread and either running stitch (page 19) for felt, or appliqué stitch (page 19) for terry cloth, sew patch to body.

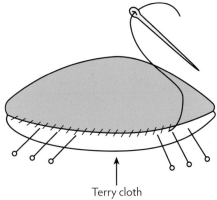

Terry cloth

❷ Using matching yarn, attach rounder, larger end of front fins directly above belly patch, a few rnds before the middle of body on each side. Attach dorsal fin to back, slightly behind front fins. Attach 1 small fin to back, a few rnds shy from end of body. Attach last 2 small fins on either side of body, directly above belly patch and in between dorsal fin and small fin on back.

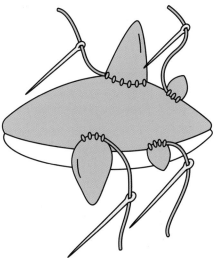

❸ For great white only: Using black yarn, apply French knots (page 18) to sides of head about 8 rnds from front of nose and 1 or 2 sts above belly patch. For non-bath toys, attach plastic eyes or sew on felt circles. (You may need to remove some stuffing temporarily to make installing safety eyes easier.) Using black yarn, apply lazy daisy sts (page 18) above eyes for eyebrows, and for 3 gills between eyes and front fins. Using black yarn, apply 1 short st on either side of nose for nostrils. Close 8-st hole and weave in end.

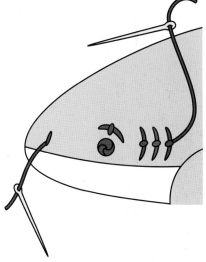

❹ For hammerhead only: Attach hammerhead eyes to front of head. Apply felt circles or follow "Hammerhead Eyes," above left, on how and when to apply plastic eyes for non-bath toys. For bath toys, apply French knots to centers of first and last rnds of hammerhead eyes. With black yarn, embroider eyebrows above eyes using lazy daisy st, and 3 gills between eyes and front fins. Close 8-st hole and weave in end.

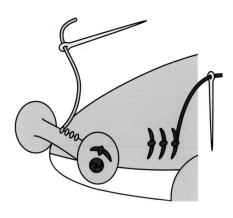

eyes, taking care to go through to crochet surface under belly patch. Sew remaining patch to belly with white thread (C).

stacked vertically with their flat sides facing you when viewed in profile. Attach larger, rounder portion of tail fins to end of shark body.

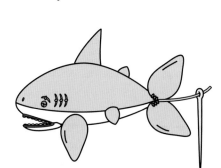

A

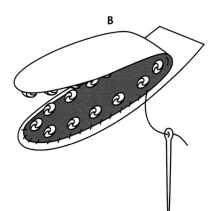

5 **For closed jaw option:** Referring to illustration for placement, draw out 1 long st (page 19) of black yarn into a loose arch shape and secure arch in place using 3 or 4 small sts over yarn in a similar manner to lazy daisy st.

B

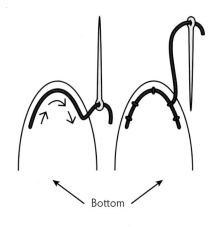

Bottom

6 **For open jaw option:** Apply white French knots around inside edge of red jaw for teeth (A). Fold jaw in half to form the top and bottom jaw. Using pattern on page 91, cut 1 mouth from either white terry cloth or felt. Sew white mouth patch to bottom half of jaw only, leaving some white fabric free to attach to shark's belly (B). Using red thread and sewing needle, sew top half of jaw to belly below

C

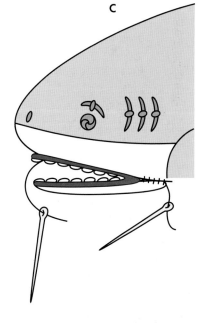

7 Position tail fins so they're

Diver

Dive into the deep with your own under-the-sea explorer! This diver is easy to customize with your favorite-colored diving suit, and the ports on the helmet will help give him or her a great view of all your amazing sea creatures!

Skill Level: Intermediate ◖■■■▭   **Finished Size:** Approx 4" wide and 6" tall

MATERIALS

- Worsted-weight yarn in orange (approx 100 yds)
- Worsted-weight yarn in skin color (approx 10 yds)
- Worsted-weight yarn in light blue (approx 10 yds)
- Worsted-weight yarn in dark brown or black (approx 5 yds)
- Size F-5 (3.75 mm) crochet hook
- Tapestry needle
- Sponge stuffing for bath toy
- For non-bath toy: 8 mm or 9 mm black plastic eyes with safety backings and toy stuffing
- Stitch markers to indicate beginning of rnds (optional)

HEAD

Using orange yarn, make an 8-st adjustable ring (page 14).

Rnd 1: Sc 2 in each sc around. (16 sts)

Rnd 2: *Sc 3, sc 2 in next sc; rep from * 3 more times. (20 sts)

Rnd 3: *Sc 1, sc 2 in next sc; rep from * 9 more times. (30 sts)

Rnd 4: *Sc 4, sc 2 in next sc; rep from * 5 more times. (36 sts)

Rnds 5–9: Sc 36.

Rnd 10: *Sc 4, sc2tog; rep from * 5 more times. (30 sts)

Rnd 11: *Sc 1, sc2tog; rep from * 9 more times. (20 sts)

Rnd 12: *Sc 3, sc2tog; rep from * 3 more times. (16 sts)

Rnd 13: Sc2tog 8 times. (8 sts)

Stuff head.

Rnd 14: *Sc 2, sc2tog; rep from * 1 more time. (6 sts)

Fasten off, leaving a long tail.

FACE

Using skin-colored yarn, make a 4-st adjustable ring.

Rnd 1: Sc 2 in each sc around. (8 sts)

Rnd 2: Sc 2 in each sc around. (16 sts)

Switch to orange yarn.

Rnd 3: In fl, sc 16.

Rnd 4: Sc 16.

Fasten off, leaving a long tail.

BODY

Using orange yarn, make an 8-st adjustable ring.

Rnd 1: Sc 2 in each sc around. (16 sts)

Rnd 2: *Sc 3, sc 2 in next st; rep from * 3 more times. (20 sts)

Rnd 3: *Sc 1, sc 2 in next st; rep from * 9 more times. (30 sts)

Rnds 4–8: Sc 30.

Rnd 9: *Sc 1, sc2tog; rep from * 9 more times. (20 sts)

Rnd 10: Sc 20.

Rnd 11: *Sc 3, sc2tog; rep from * 3 more times. (16 sts)

Stuff body.

Rnd 12: Sc2tog 8 times. (8 sts)

Rnd 13: Sc2tog 4 times. (4 sts)

Fasten off, leaving a long tail.

FOOT

Make 2.

Using orange yarn, make a 6-st adjustable ring.

Rnd 1: Sc 3, sc 2 in next sc, sc 3 in next sc, sc 2 in next sc. (10 sts)

Rnd 2: Sc 3, *sc 2 in next sc; rep from * 6 more times. (17 sts)

Rnds 3–5: Sc 17.

Rnd 6: Sc 1, sc2tog 8 times. (9 sts)

Rnds 7 and 8: Sc 9.

Stuff and fasten off. Close 9-st hole and weave in end.

NOSE

Using skin-colored yarn, make a 4-st adjustable ring.

Sl st into next sc and fasten off, leaving a long tail.

ARM

Make 2.

Using orange yarn, make a 6-st adjustable ring.

Rnd 1: Sc 3, hdc, dc, hdc. (6 sts)

Rnd 2: Sc 3, sc 2 in next sc, sc 3 in next sc, sc 2 in next sc. (10 sts)

Rnd 3: In bl, sc 10.

Rnd 4: *Sc 3, sc2tog; rep from * 1 more time. (8 sts)

Rnd 5: Sc 8.

Stuff and fasten off, leaving a long tail.

HAND

Make 2.

Using orange yarn, make a 6-st adjustable ring. Ch 1 and turn.

Sk first ch, sc, hdc, dc, hdc, sc, sl st and fasten off, leaving a long tail.

THUMB

Make 2.

Using orange yarn, loosely ch 6. Starting in 2nd ch from hook and working in back ridge lps, sc 5.

Fasten off, leaving a long tail.

PORTS

Make 4.

Using blue yarn, make a 4-st adjustable ring.

Rnd 1: Sc 2 in each sc around. (8 sts)

Switch to orange yarn.

Rnd 2: In fl, sc 8.

Rnd 3: Sc 8.

Fasten off, leaving a long tail.

BIB

Using orange yarn, loosely ch 14.

Row 1: Starting in 2nd ch from hook and working in back ridge lps, sc 2 in each ch. Ch 1 and turn. (26 sts)

Row 2: Sk ch 1, sc 26. (26 sts)

Fasten off, leaving a long tail.

BELT

Using brown yarn, loosely ch 22 to 25 (adjust to fit around diver's waist).

Fasten off, leaving a long tail.

ASSEMBLY

❶ Using orange yarn, attach face port to front of head. Using skin-colored yarn and tapestry needle, attach nose in center of face. For bath toys, using brown or black yarn and tapestry needle, apply French knots (page 18) on either side of nose for eyes. For non-bath toys, sew on felt circles or attach plastic eyes, making sure that eye posts go through both face and head layers. With brown or black yarn, embroider eyebrows above eyes using lazy daisy st (page 18) or short straight st.

❷ Using orange yarn, attach ports to sides, top, and back of head. Attach head to tapered end of body.

❸ Flatten and sew open edges of arms closed. Sew hands and thumbs to end of arms. Attach arms to body at shoulders (A). Add crochet details around cuffs as follows (see page 17): Sc onto surface of arm on rnd 3. Cont around circumference of arm until you reach first sc, sl st and fasten off (B).

❹ Using orange yarn, pull yarn through body from back to front 4 rnds from bottom of body. Loop a long st (page 19) around from front to back and rep, pulling on yarn tightly to form 2 distinctive leg shapes. Pull yarn through 1 more time and fasten off. Attach feet to bottom of legs.

❺ Place bib around neck and sew ends tog at back of head. Wrap belt around body at waist and sew ends tog in back. Thread 2 strands of orange yarn onto a tapestry needle and sew 6 evenly spaced belt loops over belt.

Pull.

Mermaid

Make a lovely mermaid or merman to splash around and make friends with all your sea creatures. For mermen, skip the shells and go a bit shorter with the hair.

Skill Level: Intermediate ■■■□ **Finished Size:** Approx 4" wide and 7" tall

MATERIALS

Worsted-weight yarn in skin color (approx 75 yds)

Worsted-weight yarn in green (approx 50 yds)

Worsted-weight yarn in turquoise (approx 50 yds)

Worsted-weight yarn in purple (approx 10 yds)

Worsted-weight yarn in brown or black (approx 5 yds)

Size F-5 (3.75 mm) crochet hook

Tapestry needle

Sponge stuffing for bath toy

For non-bath toy: 8 mm or 9 mm black plastic eyes with safety backings and toy stuffing

Stitch markers to indicate beginning of rnds (optional)

HEAD

Using skin-colored yarn, make an 8-st adjustable ring (page 14).

Rnd 1: Sc 2 in each sc around. (16 sts)

Rnd 2: *Sc 3, sc 2 in next sc; rep from * 3 more times. (20 sts)

Rnd 3: *Sc 1, sc 2 in next sc; rep from * 9 more times. (30 sts)

Rnd 4: *Sc 4, sc 2 in next sc; rep from * 5 more times. (36 sts)

Rnds 5–9: Sc 36.

Rnd 10: *Sc 4, sc2tog; rep from * 5 more times. (30 sts)

Rnd 11: *Sc 1, sc2tog; rep from * 9 more times. (20 sts)

Rnd 12: *Sc 3, sc2tog; rep from * 3 more times. (16 sts)

Rnd 13: Sc2tog 8 times. (8 sts)

Stuff head.

Rnd 14: *Sc 2, sc2tog; rep from * 1 more time. (6 sts)

Fasten off, leaving a long tail.

BODY

Using green yarn, make a 4-st adjustable ring.

Rnd 1: *Sc 1, sc 2 in next st; rep from * 1 more time. (6 sts)

Rnd 2: *Sc 2, sc 2 in next st; rep from * 1 more time. (8 sts)

Rnd 3: *Sc 1, sc 2 in next st; rep from * 3 more times. (12 sts)

Rnd 4: *Sc 2, sc 2 in next st; rep from * 3 more times. (16 sts)

Rnd 5: *Sc 3, sc 2 in next st; rep from * 3 more times. (20 sts)

Rnd 6: *Sc 1, sc 2 in next st; rep from * 9 more times. (30 sts)

Rnds 7–9: Sc 30.

Switch to skin-colored yarn.

Rnd 10: In bl, sc 30.

Rnd 11: Sc 30.

Rnd 12: *Sc 1, sc2tog; rep from * 9 more times. (20 sts)

Rnd 13: Sc 20.

Rnd 14: *Sc 3, sc2tog; rep from * 3 more times. (16 sts)

Stuff body.

Rnd 15: Sc2tog 8 times. (8 sts)

Rnd 16: Sc2tog 4 times. (4 sts)

Fasten off, leaving a long tail.

NOSE

Using skin-colored yarn, make a 4-st adjustable ring.

Sl st into next sc and fasten off, leaving a long tail.

EAR

Make 2.

Using skin-colored yarn, make a 6-st adjustable ring. Ch 1 and turn.

Sk first ch, sc 6.

Fasten off, leaving a long tail.

ARM

Make 2.

Using skin-colored yarn, make a 6-st adjustable ring.

Rnd 1: Sc 3, hdc, dc, hdc. (6 sts)

Rnd 2: Sc 3, sc 2 in next sc, sc 3 in next sc, sc 2 in next sc. (10 sts)

Rnd 3: Sc 10.

Rnd 4: *Sc 3, sc2tog; rep from * 1 more time. (8 sts)

Rnd 5: Sc 8.

Stuff. Fasten off, leaving a long tail

HAND

Make 2.

Using skin-colored yarn, make a 6-st adjustable ring. Ch 1 and turn.

Sk first ch, sc, hdc, dc, hdc, sc, sl st and fasten off, leaving a long tail.

THUMB

Make 2.

Using skin-colored yarn, loosely ch 6.

Starting in 2nd ch from hook and working in back ridge lps, sc 5.

Fasten off, leaving a long tail.

TAIL FIN

Make 2.

Using green yarn, make a 5-st adjustable ring.

Rnd 1: Sc 2 in each st around. (10 sts)

Rnd 2: *Sc 4, sc 2 in next sc; rep from * 1 more time. (12 sts)

Rnds 3 and 4: Sc 12.

Rnd 5: *Sc 1, sc2tog; rep from * 3 more times. (8 sts)

Rnd 6: Sc 8.

Rnd 7: *Sc 2, sc2tog; rep from * 1 more time. (6 sts)

Rnd 8: Sc2tog 3 times. (3 sts)

Fasten off, leaving a long tail.

SEASHELL

Make 2.

Using purple yarn, make a 6-st adjustable ring. Ch 1 and turn. Sk first ch, sc, hdc, dc, hdc, sc, sl st and fasten off, leaving a long tail.

ASSEMBLY

❶ Using skin-colored yarn and tapestry needle, attach nose to front of head. For bath toys, using brown or black yarn, apply French knots (page 18) on either side of nose. For non-bath toys, attach plastic eyes or sew on felt circles. Using turquoise yarn, embroider eyebrows above eyes using lazy daisy st (page 18). Attach ears to sides of head.

❷ Using turquoise yarn, attach hair (see "Crocheting on the Surface" on page 17).

Row 1: Using illustrations as a guide, sc onto surface of head in a spiral starting at top of head and cont this line of sts onto back of head in an S-like pattern. Ch 1 and turn.

Front   Back

Row 2: Sk first ch, *sl st in next sc and ch 6 to 8 (or more for longer hair). Starting in 2nd ch from hook and working in back ridge lps, sc 2 in each ch, sl st in next sc on row 1; rep from * until you reach last sc at top of head, adjusting length of chs as you go. Sl st in last sc and fasten off. Weave in yarn end.

❸ Using skin-colored yarn, attach head, taking care to orient the location of the color-change transition on body to back of toy. Starting at back of toy and using green yarn, sc on surface of body into each of front lps of the color transition rnd (rnd 10) of body. Once you've gone around waist once, join first and last sc tog with sl st.

4 Flatten and sew open edges of arms tog. Sew on hand and thumbs to end of arms. Attach arms to body at shoulders. Attach tail fins.

5 To shape seashells, pinch and sew bottom of piece tog to create teardrop shape. Attach seashells to front of body. Using purple yarn, apply long sts between shells and around back of body to create sea-shell bikini ties. Then make small sts over the ties to hold them in place.

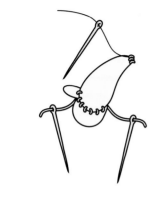

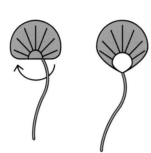

Patterns

You can print templates directly from MKcrochet.com/resources or from ShopMartingale.com/extras. For terry-cloth patches, cut out pattern on solid black lines. For felt patches, cut out patterns on dotted lines and sew darts together on the wrong side of the patch where indicated before applying the patches to your toy.

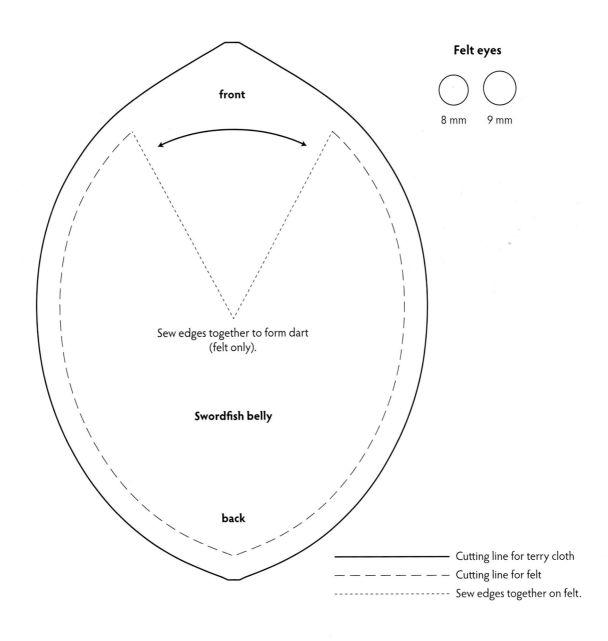

front

Felt eyes

8 mm   9 mm

Sew edges together to form dart
(felt only).

Swordfish belly

back

———————— Cutting line for terry cloth

– – – – – – – Cutting line for felt

·········· Sew edges together on felt.

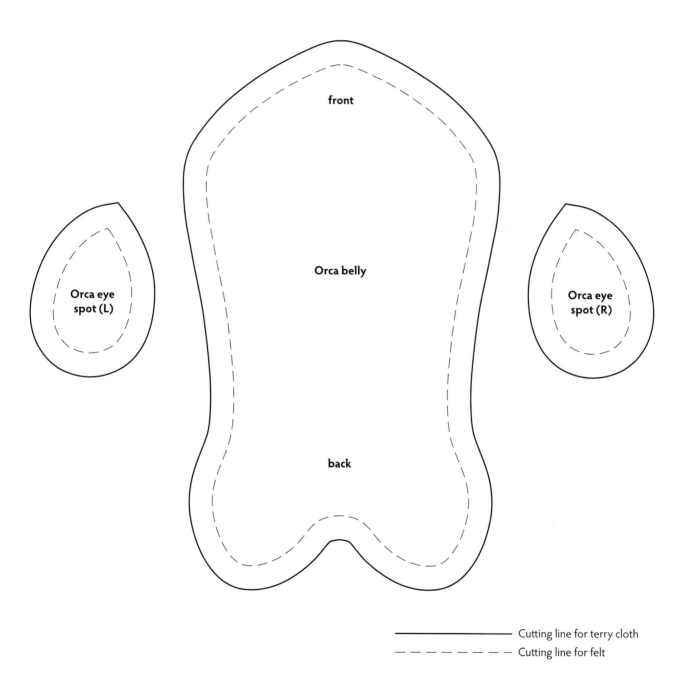

front

Orca belly

back

Orca eye
spot (L)

Orca eye
spot (R)

Cutting line for terry cloth
Cutting line for felt

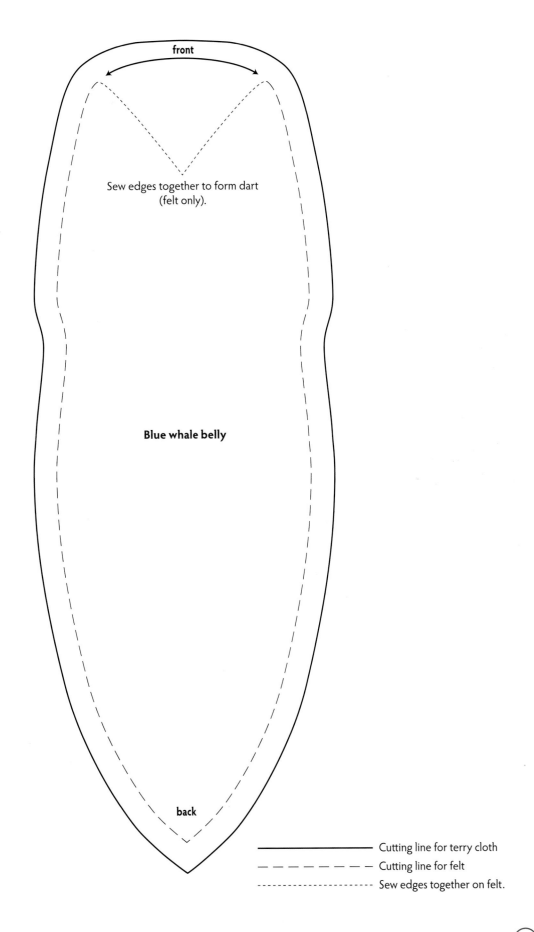

front

Sew edges together to form dart
(felt only).

Blue whale belly

back

Cutting line for terry cloth
Cutting line for felt
Sew edges together on felt.

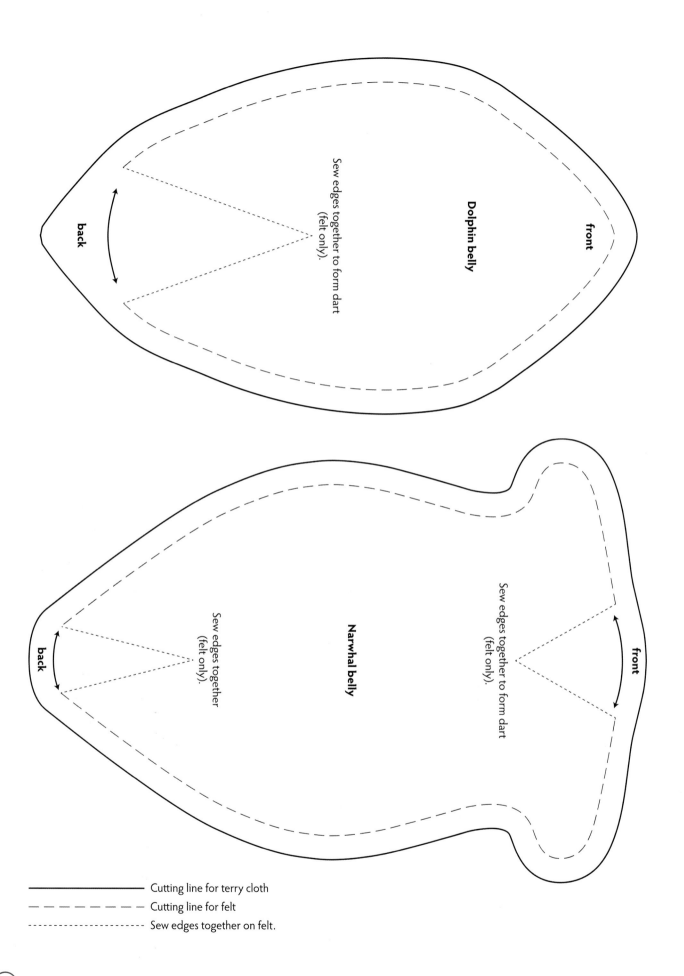

Sew edges together to form dart (felt only).

Dolphin belly

front

back

Sew edges together (felt only).

Narwhal belly

Sew edges together to form dart (felt only).

front

back

——————— Cutting line for terry cloth

– – – – – Cutting line for felt

· · · · · · · Sew edges together on felt.

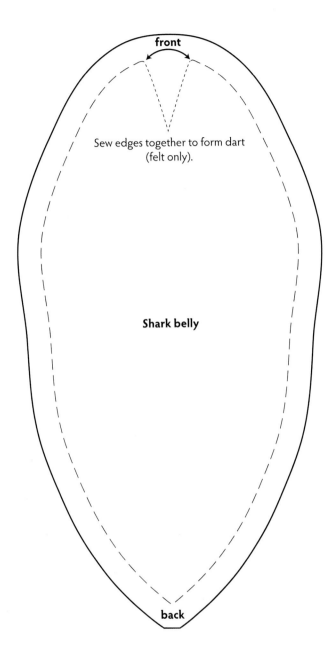

front

Sew edges together to form dart
(felt only).

Shark belly

back

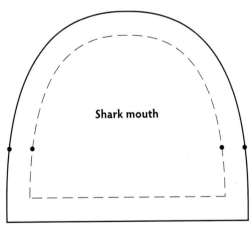

Shark mouth

**Sew curved edge from dot to dot to bottom of jaw.
Sew corners and straight edge from dot to dot to belly.
Adjust as needed.**

―――――――――― Cutting line for terry cloth

― ― ― ― ― ― Cutting line for felt

----------------------- Sew edges together on felt.

Useful Information

STANDARD YARN WEIGHTS

Yarn-Weight Symbol and Category Name	1 Super Fine	2 Fine	3 Light	4 Medium	5 Bulky	6 Super Bulky
Types of Yarn in Category	Sock, Fingering, Baby	Sport, Baby	DK, Light Worsted	Worsted, Afghan, Aran	Chunky, Craft, Rug	Bulky, Roving
Crochet Gauge* Range in Single Crochet to 4"	21 to 32 sts	16 to 20 sts	12 to 17 sts	11 to 14 sts	8 to 11 sts	5 to 9 sts
Recommended Hook in Metric Size Range	2.25 to 3.5 mm	3.5 to 4.5 mm	4.5 to 5.5 mm	5.5 to 6.5 mm	6.5 to 9 mm	9 mm and larger
Recommended Hook in U.S. Size Range	B-1 to E-4	E-4 to 7	7 to I-9	I-9 to K-10½	K-10½ to M-13	M-13 and larger

*These are guidelines only. The above reflect the most commonly used gauges and hook sizes for specific yarn categories.

SKILL LEVELS

■□□□ **Beginner:** Projects for first-time crocheters using basic stitches; minimal shaping.

■■□□ **Easy:** Projects using yarn with basic stitches, repetitive stitch patterns, simple color changes, and simple shaping and finishing.

■■■□ **Intermediate:** Projects using a variety of techniques, such as basic lace patterns or color patterns; midlevel shaping and finishing.

■■■■ **Experienced:** Projects with intricate stitch patterns, techniques, and dimension, such as non-repeating patterns, multicolor techniques, fine threads, small hooks, detailed shaping, and refined finishing.

CROCHET HOOK SIZES

Millimeter	US Size*
2.25 mm	B-1
2.75 mm	C-2
3.25 mm	D-3
3.5 mm	E-4
3.75 mm	F-5
4 mm	G-6
4.5 mm	7
5 mm	H-8
5.5 mm	I-9
6 mm	J-10
6.5 mm	K-10 1/2
8 mm	L-11
9 mm	M/N-13

*Letter or number may vary. Rely on the millimeter sizing.

Resources

If you're interested in using some of the yarns or tools
in this book, please check out the following resources.

Coats and Clark
www.coatsandclark.com
Red Heart Yarns, available at local
craft stores

Lion Brand
www.lionbrandyarn.com
Cotton-Ease yarn, available at local
craft stores

Knit Picks
www.knitpicks.com
Dishie yarn, available online.

Hobbs Bonded Fibers
www.hobbsbondedfibers.com
Poly-down fiberfill toy stuffing and
black batting, available at local
craft stores

NearSea Naturals
www.nearseanaturals.com
Online retailer of sustainable, natural, and organic stuffing and thread

6060
www.6060.etsy.com
Online retailer of unique plastic
safety eyes

Clover
www.clover-usa.com
Hooks and notions, available at
local craft stores

Fiskars
www.fiskars.com
Scissors and cutting mats, available
at local craft stores

Fabric.com
www.fabric.com
Online fabric retailer

American Felt and Craft
www.americanfeltandcraft.com
Online retailer of fine wool felts
and toy noise-maker inserts

Summer Infant
www.summerinfant.com
Maker of Summer Infant Comfy
Bath Sponge, available on
Amazon.com

Yarns Used

Guppies

<u>Orange Guppy</u>

Lion Brand Martha Stewart Cotton Hemp in Black Licorice (553), Clementine (533), and Sour Cherry (513)

<u>Yellow Guppy</u>

Lion Brand Martha Stewart Cotton Hemp in Lemon Drop (557), Black Licorice (553), and Clementine (533)

<u>Purple Guppy</u>

Lion Brand Martha Stewart Cotton Hemp in Sugared Violet (544), Heather Flower (546), and Black Licorice (553)

<u>Blue Guppy</u>

Lion Brand Martha Stewart Cotton Hemp in Blue Icing (506), Peacock (578), and Black Licorice (553)

Starfish

Lion Brand Kitchen Cotton in Cayenne (114), Vanilla (98), Kiwi (170), and Blue Ice (108)

Stingray

Lion Brand Cotton-Ease in Taupe (122), Almond (099), and Charcoal (152)

Jellyfish

<u>Orange Jellyfish</u>

Red Heart Creme de la Creme in Brite Orange (0252), Rally Red (0905), and Orangetones (0945)

<u>Pink Jellyfish</u>

Red Heart Creme de la Creme in Pretty in Pink (0970), Orchid Pink (0701), and Brite Pink (0720)

<u>Blue Jellyfish</u>

Red Heart Creme de la Creme in Royal Blue (0887), Cornflower Blue (0870, and Denim Ombre (0980)

<u>White Jellyfish</u>

Red Heart Creme de la Creme in White (0001), Mints (0628), and Pastels Ombre (0970)

<u>Purple Jellyfish</u>

Red Heart Creme de la Crème in White (0001), Snow Violet Ombre (0993), and Wood Violet (0910)

Seahorses

<u>Green Seahorse</u>

Red Heart Creme de la Creme in Black (0012), Minty (0628), and Arizona Ombre (0933)

<u>Pink Seahorse</u>

Red Heart Creme de la Creme in Black (0012), Orchid Pink (0701), and Cherry Blossom (0934)

<u>Yellow Seahorse</u>

Red Heart Creme de la Creme in Black (0012), Golden Yellow (0205), and Goldtones (0960)

Sea Turtle

Red Heart Creme de la Creme in Cream (0101), Brite Green (0625), Forest (049), and Black (0012)

Angler Fish

Lion Brand Kitchen Cotton in Grape (147), Vanilla (98), and Licorice (153)

Octopus

Lion Brand Cotton-Ease in Terracotta (134), Almond (099), and Charcoal (152)

Manatee

Knit Picks Dishie in Silver (25789)

Red Heart Creme de la Creme in Black (0012)

Sea Otter

Red Heart Creme de la Creme in Fudge Brown (0331), Black (0012), Linen (0118), and Gray (0400)

Lobster

Lion Brand Cotton-Ease in Cherry (113) and Charcoal (152)

Blue Crab

Lion Brand Cotton-Ease in Stone (149), Almond (099), Seaspray (123), Terracotta (134), and Charcoal (152)

Swordfish

Lion Brand Kitchen Cotton in Blueberry (106), Vanilla (98), and Licorice (153)

Dolphin

Red Heart Creme de la Creme in Tile Blue (0810) and Black (0012)

Narwhal

Lion Brand Cotton-Ease in Charcoal (152) and Stone (149)

Blue Whale

Lion Brand Cotton-Ease in Turquoise (148) and Charcoal (152)

Orca

Red Heart Creme de la Creme in Black (0012)

Lion Brand Cotton-Ease in Charcoal (152)

Sharks

<u>Great White</u>

Red Heart Creme de la Creme in Grey (0400) and Black (0012)

<u>Hammerhead</u>

Red Heart Creme de la Creme in DK Linen (035)

<u>Shark Mouth</u>

Red Heart Creme de la Creme in White (0001) and Scarlet (0906)

Diver

Knit Picks Dishie in Clementine (25403), Azure (25412), Flamingo (25407), and Coffee (25399)

Mermaid

Knit Picks Dishie in Linen (25400), Kenai (25788), Aster (25413), Tranquil (25405), and Coffee (25399)

Abbreviations

*	Repeat instructions following the asterisk(s) as directed		rep(s)	repeat(s)
approx	approximately		rnd(s)	round(s)
beg	begin(ning)		RS	right side
bl	back loop(s)		sc	single crochet(s)
CC	contrasting color		sc2tog	single crochet 2 stitches together—1 stitch decreased.
ch(s)	chain(s) or chain stitch(es)		sk	skip
cont	continue(ing)(s)		sl	slip
dc	double crochet(s)		sl st(s)	slip stitch(es)
fl	front loop(s)		st(s)	stitch(es)
hdc	half double crochet(s)		tog	together
lp(s)	loop(s)		tr	triple crochet
MC	main color		WS	wrong side
mm	millimeter		yd(s)	yard(s)

ACKNOWLEDGMENTS

It was through the amazing support of friends, family, and the publishing team at Martingale that this book was made possible. Thank you to the following:

My husband, Michael, for letting me take over our dining room table as I went through the pattern writing process all over again, and for the amazing support you've given to me during all my yarn-fueled endeavors (regardless of the scale or complexity).

My parents, who nurtured my love of art since I could hold a pencil (or a crochet hook).

Ursula Reikes and Marcy Heffernan, for taking such amazing care in editing and checking over all the patterns.

Paula Schlosser, Brent Kane, Connor Chin, Sue Mattero, and Cheryl Fall for creating such a beautiful look for the book.

Karen Burns, Karen Soltys, and Mary Green, for giving me the opportunity to publish my first book and for promptly asking me to write a second one.

And, finally, to my children, James and Emily, who continue to inspire me to be creative every day.

About the Author

Photograph by David Hoffmann

Megan Kreiner grew up on Long Island, New York, in a household where art and art projects were a daily part of life. Coming from a long line of knitters and crocheters, Megan learned the craft at an early age from her grandmother, her aunt, and her mother. She started designing crochet patterns in 2011 under the name "MK Crochet" (www.mkcrochet.com).

A graduate with a fine arts degree in computer graphics and animation from the University of Massachusetts, Amherst, Megan is pursuing a career in the feature animation industry in Los Angeles. She is an animator at DreamWorks Animation SKG.

Megan lives in Altadena, California, with her husband, Michael, and their children, James and Emily.

mk crochet ®

Photograph by Julie Rollins Photography

What's your creative passion?

Find it at ShopMartingale.com

books • eBooks • ePatterns • daily blog • free projects
videos • tutorials • inspiration • giveaways

Martingale
Create with Confidence